What They Didn't Tell You about Knowledge Management

Jay Liebowitz

THE SCARECROW PRESS, INC.
Lanham, Maryland • Toronto • Oxford
2006

SCARECROW PRESS, INC.

Published in the United States of America
by Scarecrow Press, Inc.
A wholly owned subsidiary of
The Rowman & Littlefield Publishing Group, Inc.
4501 Forbes Boulevard, Suite 200, Lanham, Maryland 20706
www.scarecrowpress.com

PO Box 317
Oxford
OX2 9RU, UK

British Library Cataloguing in Publication Information Available

Library of Congress Cataloging-in-Publication Data

Liebowitz, Jay.
  What they didn't tell you about knowledge management / Jay Liebowitz.
      p. cm.
  Includes index.
  ISBN-13: 978-0-8108-5725-4 (pbk. : alk. paper)
  ISBN-10: 0-8108-5725-1 (pbk. : alk. paper)
  1. Knowledge management. I. Title.
HD30.2.L53 2006
658.4'038—dc22   2005034302

♾™ The paper used in this publication meets the minimum requirements of American
National Standard for Information Sciences—Permanence of Paper for Printed Library
Materials, ANSI/NISO Z39.48-1992.
Manufactured in the United States of America.

Contents

Preface

A myriad of books have been published on knowledge management over the years. Yet very few provide practical guidance to information and library science professionals to make knowledge management (KM) a success in their organizations.

This book strives to accomplish this goal. It is a concise guide based on many years of experience in the knowledge management field. It is intended for information and library science professionals, managers, business executives, knowledge management professionals, human capital officers, IT professionals, HR (human resources) managers, and students/educators/practitioners interested in KM.

In developing this book, I tried to address the typical questions and issues facing information and library science professionals as they embark on their KM journey. I had many of the same questions when I began my KM adventure, and over the years I have been able to apply the lessons I've learned (which are contained in this book) to ensure my organization's KM success.

I hope you enjoy reading the book as much as I enjoyed writing it. Have fun!

Acknowledgments

To my wonderful family—Janet, Jason, Kenny, and Mazel—for enduring my constant muttering of "I'm on chapter . . ." To my mother, Marilyn, who can't believe I'm writing yet another book! To all my supportive colleagues at Johns Hopkins University for their insight and good humor. To my thousands of students I've taught over the last twenty-three years—what a privilege! And, finally, to Martin, Kellie, and Ed at Scarecrow Press for allowing me to share my knowledge and catharsis.

Chapter One

The Management Fad of the Day

TQM, TQL, BPR, BPI, CRM, and now KM?

Over the years we've played alphabet soup with a host of management theories and practices. Acronyms have long played a role in our everyday lives. Some people believe that many of these acronyms are fraught with the inherent peculiarities of the times and that the next "management fad" will be created to pick up where we left off.

Here are a few of these so-called fads. TQM stands for Total Quality Management. Certainly, the underlying principles of TQM are relevant and have allowed organizations to improve their productivity, efficiency, and effectiveness. However, many people don't like to be "measured," and TQM is heavily immersed in measurement. Then TQL (Total Quality Leadership) became an extension of TQM to explain the crucial role leaders have in the quality approach. The quality movement led to the BPR (Business Process Reengineering) and BPI (Business Process Improvement) efforts, whereby organizations examined their business processes and tried to improve them in order to increase their effectiveness. Again, the central theme was that people and their related processes were being measured, which runs counter to most people's preferences. Anecdotally, Michael Hammer (who developed BPR) and others have stated that BPR and BPI efforts have generally failed—about a 70 percent failure rate. Then the CRM (Customer Relationship Management) movement gained momentum, and organizations were trying to maximize their outreach and leverage their knowledge externally with customers and stakeholders. CRM was still an important part of the organizational fabric, but the concepts were extended to look at leveraging and sharing knowledge internally as well as externally. This gave rise to the KM (Knowledge Management) community, which has its roots in information and library sciences, organizational learning, human resources management, information technology, and strategic management. KM has now become a key pillar in many organizations' strategic human capital plans.

The list of acronyms goes on—BI (Business Intelligence), CI (Competitive Intelligence), SI (Strategic Intelligence)—and it's no wonder that the typical employee is confused and overwhelmed. It's easier to just say, "This is a passing fad, and I'll just ride the waves for a while until we get new leadership or until something else comes along." However, knowledge management is a bit different than its predecessors. Most senior leaders can appreciate knowledge management for its value in terms of maximizing their organization's competitive edge through their key asset—their people. KM has a more intangible, long-lasting nature than earlier techniques. Of course, its intangibility makes senior leadership quiver, as it's difficult to quantify.

I've developed a set of key reasons and benefits to explain why organizations embark on a quest for knowledge management and then apply those principles. These are categorized into the following sections:

Adaptability/Agility

- Anticipating potential market opportunities for new products/services
- Rapidly commercializing new innovations
- Adapting quickly to unanticipated changes
- Anticipating surprises and crises
- Quickly adapting the organization's goals and objectives to industry/market changes
- Decreasing market response times
- Being responsive to new market demands
- Learning, deciding, and adapting faster than the competition

Creativity

- Innovating new products/services
- Identifying new business opportunities
- Learning not to reinvent the wheel
- Quickly accessing and building on experience and ideas to fuel innovation

Institutional Memory Building

- Attracting and retaining employees
- Retaining expertise of personnel
- Capturing and sharing best practices

Organizational *Internal* Effectiveness

- Coordinating the development efforts of different units
- Increasing the sense of belonging and community among employees in the organization
- Avoiding overlapping the development of corporate initiatives
- Streamlining the organization's internal processes
- Reducing redundancy of information and knowledge
- Improving profits and increasing revenues
- Shortening product development cycles
- Providing training and corporate learning
- Accelerating the transfer and use of existing know-how
- Improving communication and coordination across company units (i.e.. reduce "stovepiping")

Organizational *External* Effectiveness

- Searching for new information about the industry and market
- Increasing customer satisfaction
- Supporting e-business initiatives
- Managing customer relationships
- Delivering competitive intelligence
- Enhancing supply chain management
- Improving strategic alliances

Some of these KM benefits can be measured. but many of them are more amorphous. Chapter 7 will explain how to show value from knowledge management initiatives.

KNOWLEDGE MANAGEMENT AND KNOWLEDGE ROLES

Knowledge management is the process of creating value from an organization's intangible assets. Knowledge management is concerned with four major types of capital. The first is human capital—the brainpower of the employees and management. Structural capital, the second type. deals with knowledge-laden items that you can't easily take home from the office. such as intellectual property rights or certain databases. Customer or social (relationship) capital deals with knowledge acquired from customers and stakeholders. The fourth, and newest. type of capital in the KM definition is competitive capital. This relates to knowledge learned about and from an organization's competitors. All four types of capital together make up knowledge management.

Some people say that KM means looking down your office hallways and CI (Competitive Intelligence) means looking out your office windows. However you define these terms, the key point is that organizations need to leverage knowledge both internally *and* externally.

In order for an organization to move forward in its knowledge management plans, knowledge roles for the various employees in the organization need to be established and modeled after the knowledge management processes. Table 1.1 shows some important roles that employees at various levels in an organization should fulfill in order to transform the entity into a "knowledge organization."

LESSONS LEARNED

When serving as the first knowledge management officer at NASA's Goddard Space Flight Center, I learned some valuable lessons that can help organizations use knowledge management effectively. First, it is easier to apply knowledge management strategies that fit an organization's culture than to change the organization's culture. Academic studies indicate that it takes ten to fourteen years to change the culture of a large organization. In order to show some quick wins from KM to overcome any possible skepticism, we don't have the luxury of time to wait for the organization's culture to change before applying KM. Use knowledge management strategically by aligning it with the particular subculture where it will be used. This will eliminate some of the resistance to change and will allow KM to have a greater likelihood of success.

Second, don't try to do everything at once. Develop a knowledge management strategic plan for the organization, and then have a two-to-three-year knowledge management implementation plan to carry out the strategy. For example, at Goddard, we had a two-year knowledge management implementation plan whereby the first year was devoted to creating an awareness of KM at all levels of the organization, educating people on KM, initiating quick-win KM pilots with metrics for success throughout the organization, developing the technology infrastructure to support knowledge sharing, and incorporating KM into the organization's human capital strategy. The second year was devoted to developing the organizational infrastructure to support knowledge management, embedding KM processes into the daily work activities of the employees, developing a recognition and reward system to promote knowledge-sharing behaviors, and expanding the KM pilots into full-fledged KM projects.

Table 1.1. Knowledge Roles (Adapted from the Work of J. Liebowitz and M. Berens at ASID)

	Director	Professional	Admin/Support
Knowledge Identification & Capture			
Identify knowledge	• Identify areas of knowledge that the organization needs to capture. • Identify knowledge and knowledge competencies needed to accomplish strategic goals. • Identify knowledge deliverables from major projects or efforts.	• Identify sources for capturing knowledge as assigned. • Identify emerging issues/trends within or affecting assigned organization segments.	• Alert staff to urgent and emerging service issues.
Capture knowledge	• Establish policies for managing knowledge and quality standards for knowledge work. • Establish schedules for knowledge capture and reporting. • Monitor knowledge contributions of assigned staff for quality and frequency.	• Monitor knowledge sources and compile relevant knowledge as assigned. • Capture lessons learned and successful practices from major projects and make them available on the intranet. • Monitor and collect information from chat rooms and threaded discussions to help identify issues for future research, online communities, and product/service offerings.	• Record and compile job-related data and information as assigned. • Report lessons learned and successful practices. • Post on the intranet and update as necessary relevant information and documentation for operating unit, as assigned.
Knowledge Sharing			
Communicate knowledge	• Facilitate open communication and	• Provide key stakeholders with regular updates/progress	• Ensure that others receive timely and useful

(continued)

Table 1.1. (continued)

	Director	Professional	Admin/Support
	knowledge sharing throughout the organization. • Provide key stakeholders with regular updates/progress reports on major projects. • Ensure that others receive timely and useful communiqués of information and knowledge they need to perform effectively.	reports on major projects/efforts. • Ensure that others receive timely and useful communiqués of information and knowledge they need to perform effectively.	communiqués of information and knowledge they need to perform effectively.
Build and nurture a knowledge-sharing culture	• Establish cross-functional project teams and foster collaboration. • Recognize and reward knowledge sharing, creation, and use. • Encourage and facilitate in-time, on-the-job learning and skill transfer. • Practice and promote knowledge sharing across the enterprise.	• Establish or participate in communities of interest, communities of practice, or other informal knowledge-sharing groups. • Respond promptly to requests for knowledge or subject-matter expertise, making sure that the response meets the requestor's need. • Acknowledge when others share knowledge.	• Respond promptly to requests for knowledge or subject-matter expertise, making sure that the response meets the requestor's need. • Acknowledge when others share knowledge.

Knowledge Application

Incorporate knowledge	• Adjust strategy, as needed, based on emerging knowledge. • Ground decision making in explicit knowledge. • Review evaluations of products, services, and programs periodically and adjust offerings accordingly.	• Gather relevant knowledge objects and assemble necessary expertise to achieve project goals. • Look for ways to add and use new knowledge to existing or new products, services, and programs. • Recommend modifications to projects or tasks, when needed, based on emerging knowledge. • Contribute suggestions for new products, services, and process improvements.	• Recommend modifications to procedures or tasks, when needed, based on emerging knowledge. • Contribute suggestions for new products, services, and process improvements.
Reuse knowledge	• Maintain and refer to "organizational memory" of how strategy was set or decisions reached.	• Consult intranet and other knowledge resources to review lessons learned and proven practices when undertaking new projects/efforts. • Use templates and other preformatted materials.	• Use templates and other preformatted materials.

(continued)

Table 1.1. (*continued*)

	Director	Professional	Admin/Support
Knowledge Creation			
Create knowledge	• Communicate, reinforce, and clearly link to projects and activities the organization's vision, mission, and goals to provide context for knowledge application and learning. • Identify and synthesize key learnings and report to leadership.	• Analyze and synthesize knowledge captured, as assigned, and share learnings. • Build and refresh content knowledge and subject-matter expertise.	• Transfer "new" knowledge into the knowledge repositories on the intranet and website, as assigned.

Third, apply knowledge management to the core competencies of the organization and show value-added benefits. At Goddard, for example, developing satellite missions and projects is one of the core areas. Once knowledge management was injected into these projects, stories could then be told about how knowledge management helped to improve productivity or increase collaboration to achieve results and mission success. When employees on other projects heard these stories, then they would often want to apply KM as well, in order to better achieve their own goals.

Fourth, any initiative will always face skeptics. Some people may feel that knowledge management is the management fad of the day. Others will see the real value that knowledge management may bring to the organization. Link up with the KM advocates early on to build a cadre of KM spokespersons. This can be done by creating a KM working group (composed of advocates from across the organization, as we had at Goddard) and by having the support of senior leadership (who typically seem to appreciate the value of knowledge management and human capital in an organization). It is also important to use both bottom-up and top-down strategies to gain support for KM. Exciting those in the working levels of the organization on the virtues of KM will encourage them to tell their managers, who will in turn tell their leaders. A top-down approach is also helpful so that the employees see that there is high-level sponsorship and support for KM activities.

Try not to force-fit solutions to requirements. In other words, try to find out the "pains" of the organization in terms of business needs and then see how knowledge management might be able to address those pains.

CASE STUDY: WHAT CAN BE LEARNED FROM A KM OPERATIONAL STUDY AT A LARGE FOUNDATION?

I conducted a knowledge management operational study at a large foundation in summer 2001. Interviews were held with key members of the foundation, and a survey of knowledge-sharing effectiveness was distributed. There was a 54 percent response rate on the survey. The survey looked at four main areas: communications flow, KM environment, organizational facilitation, and measurement. "Communications flow" dealt with how knowledge and communication exchanges were captured and disseminated throughout the organization. "Knowledge management environment" looked at internal cultural factors related to knowledge management within the organization. "Organizational facilitation" assessed the sophistication of the knowledge management infrastructure and knowledge-sharing capability within the organization. "Measurement" assessed the likelihood of knowledge sharing and knowledge management being successful within the organization.

The survey results showed that the foundation was performing at a C (average) level on a scale from A to F. Strategies for improvement identified in the "communications flow" category were: enhance the foundation's codification strategy in terms of capturing key expertise in an online way; direct (via intelligent agent technology, or software that acts without human intervention) lessons learned and best practices to individuals in the organization who could benefit from these lessons; and transform individualized learning into organizational learning. In terms of the knowledge management environment, the study showed that the foundation should consider a formal mentoring program to improve the sharing and exchange of tacit knowledge and encourage a knowledge-sharing culture. Systematic job rotations could also be used to encourage a better understanding of the foundation's core activities and to promote interdisciplinary dialogue. In terms of organizational facilitation of knowledge management capability, the foundation should consider revising its motivation and reward system to include learning and knowledge-sharing criteria (as is done at the World Bank and other organizations). In order to nurture a knowledge-sharing culture, the foundation should consider systematically collecting success, failure, and war stories on their intranet and should use storytelling as a means for knowledge sharing. For example, for the first ten to fifteen minutes of regular staff meetings, people could exchange stories that might help others at the foundation. Only 15 percent of respondents felt that they typically reused knowledge gained from others in the foundation. The study concluded that by promoting a knowledge-sharing culture via storytelling at staff meetings, recognizing people who share what they know and rewarding them, encoding best practices and lessons learned on their intranet (see, for example, the NASA Lessons Learned Information System at llis.nasa .gov), encouraging the use of online communities, and continuing the use of cross-functional teams, the foundation could see dramatic changes in individual and organizational behavior that would transform it into a "knowledge organization."

Peter Senge feels that five key disciplines are needed for an organization to truly be a "learning organization": systems thinking, personal mastery, mental models, building shared vision, and team learning. Senge, in his book *The Fifth Discipline*, states that "organizations need to be good at knowledge generation, appropriation and exploitation—this process is not that easy." In his 2001 book *Good to Great*, Jim Collins found that eleven "great" companies had a common characteristic: a Level 5 leader. In Collins's work, a Level 5 leader is an executive in whom extreme personal humility blends paradoxically with intense professional will. Thus, leadership (and followership) is a critical element in transforming an organization into a learning organization.

A TWO-YEAR KNOWLEDGE MANAGEMENT IMPLEMENTATION PLAN FOR THE FOUNDATION

In my study of the foundation. I recommended that the organization follow a two-year implementation plan of its knowledge management strategy. In the first year, the following should be done:

- Create an awareness of knowledge management at all levels in the foundation.
- Educate foundation employees and management on knowledge management.
- Conduct a knowledge audit and knowledge mapping of the foundation.
- Initiate quick-win, knowledge management pilots with metrics for success throughout the foundation (e.g., an expertise locator. online communities, best-practice/lessons-learned repositories).
- Spawn one or two external online communities with active facilitators.
- Develop the technology infrastructure to support knowledge sharing.
- Incorporate knowledge management into the foundation's human capital strategy, including the following key pillars: competency management, performance management, knowledge management, and change management.

In the second year, the following should be done:

- Develop the organizational infrastructure to support knowledge management (e.g., knowledge stewards and knowledge retention managers).
- Embed knowledge management processes into the daily working activities of the employees (e.g., capture and share lessons learned during each phase of the project life cycle, encourage storytelling at staff meetings).
- Develop a recognition and reward system to promote knowledge sharing.
- Expand the knowledge management pilots into full-fledged knowledge management projects and measure their success.
- Apply proactive techniques for knowledge sharing (e.g., pushing "new" knowledge, best practices, and lessons learned via intelligent agent technology to the community).
- Spawn another four or five online communities, with active facilitators, on pertinent knowledge areas for their target audiences.

After the first two years of the knowledge management implementation plan. a formal evaluation should be conducted by a team composed of representatives of the foundation. representatives of the user community. selected knowledge management specialists, and external examiners. Based upon this formal evaluation, a knowledge management implementation plan for the following two to three years could then be established.

SUMMARY

Knowledge management is gradually being woven into the fabric of organizations. In many cases, it is being integrated as one of the key pillars underpinning an organization's human capital strategy. Knowledge management will probably never be a discipline similar to the hard or soft sciences. However, KM has significant value in the longevity of organizations, especially as it relates to organizational learning. Even though more rigor needs to be put into KM so that it becomes more science and less art, knowledge management will always provide ways of building community, increasing innovation, and facilitating knowledge retention in organizations.

REFERENCES

Collins, J. (2001). *Good to Great*. Eastbourne, England, Gardners Books.
Senge, P. (1990). *The Fifth Discipline: The Art and Practice of the Learning Organization*. Currency, New York.

Chapter Two

Gaining the Knowledge behind Knowledge Management

In Wesley Vestal's article "Making Sense Out of KM Costs" (2005), he discusses the Open Standards Benchmarking Collaborative Research effort, organized by APQC (formerly the American Productivity and Quality Center), which examines the structure and roles of knowledge management, stages of KM implementation, KM costs and budgets, KM program measures and outcomes, knowledge-sharing processes, and KM content and technology. In a survey of forty-three organizations, 83 percent indicated that they had a formal knowledge management program in place. "Formal" meant that there is a dedicated budget for KM, at least one full-time employee supports KM activities, and KM is recognized by the organization as an initiative. Whether having a formal or informal KM program, organizations found that they needed to have an initial business case with specific goals, a vision, and a defined budget. About 46.2 percent of the respondents spent at least $1 million on a formal KM approach, and about 57.2 percent of the respondents with an informal KM program spent less than $500,000. Over half of the respondents indicated that the KM program was enterprise-wide or centrally managed. About 75 percent of the respondents had designated KM roles within business units. Most organizations used a variety of approaches for applying KM rather than a single solution. The top knowledge management approaches (used by at least 50 percent of the respondents) were, in order: communities of practice, best-practice transfer, content management systems, lessons-learned programs, and knowledge retention efforts. Few organizations had fully institutionalized KM in their annual performance reviews. About 62 percent of the respondents utilized an explicit communication process to share information about tools and KM successes.

After painting this KM picture, we can see that knowledge management seems to be a part of the inner fabric of many organizations. As mentioned in the previous chapter, knowledge management is being subsumed within organizations in various ways. One approach is to use knowledge management as part of an organization's human capital strategy. In the U.S. government, agencies are following a model developed by the Office of Personnel Management (OPM), the Office of Management and Budget (OMB), and the Government Accountability Office (GAO) that includes a "Leadership and Knowledge Management" pillar as part of a framework for the strategic management of human capital. Other organizations are implementing knowledge management under the direction of a chief knowledge officer, a chief learning officer, a director of intellectual capital, or the equivalent. And still others are integrating knowledge management through their human resources, information technology, organizational development, strategic planning, or library and information sciences departments. Depending upon where KM is housed, different approaches will be used—as I will explain next.

CODIFICATION AND PERSONALIZATION

Most organizations will apply both a systems-oriented "collection" approach (codification) and a people-to-people "connection" approach (personalization) to KM, but one of these two methods will dominate. We have always had the "collection" approach, but now with web-based technologies and intranets, we can build bridges across isolated islands of knowledge. Each island, called a "silo" or a "stovepipe" in organizational parlance, often operates and communicates in isolation from others. These functional silos are artifacts from the many years that a particular organization has existed. Knowledge management offers a way to integrate these functional silos so that communications, innovation, and productivity can be enhanced.

In selecting a codification or a personalization approach, a key determinant is the existing organizational culture. For example, if an organization has a large percentage of ISTJs (Introverted, Sensing, Thinking, and Judging types based on the Myers-Briggs Type Indicator test), then these individuals may feel more comfortable with the systems-oriented codification approach to knowledge management. If, on the other hand, many employees enjoy interacting with each other and are entrepreneurial types, then the personalization approach to KM may be effective, because it supports the way the people work in the organization. This is not to suggest that an organization should use one approach to the exclusion of another. Rather, the 80-20 rule applies, and the major KM approach selected should typically be aligned with the organizational culture.

For example, NASA's Goddard Space Flight Center was using codification as their major KM approach. Many of the employees were scientists, engineers, and technologists, so they were used to a systems perspective, and many were ISTJs. Codification techniques included having lessons-learned databases, searchable online video repositories, expert locator systems, "knowledge nuggets," and the like. Personalization approaches were also used—Creative Learning Groups, online communities of practice, knowledge-sharing forums, job rotations, job shadowing, mentoring, and cross-functional teams—but the codification approach dominated. The following are the next steps that were recommended to turn Goddard into a "knowledge organization."

- Use the Knowledge Management Working Group as the Goddard knowledge management steering committee to facilitate development and ongoing nurturing of knowledge management efforts.
- Develop online knowledge management systems, strategically placed within the center, that will include best and worst practices, lessons learned, frequently asked questions and answers, appropriate documentation, cases, and online pools of mission-critical knowledge that have been elicited from experts within the center.
- Build and nurture online communities of practice (personalization approach).
- Map experts to knowledge areas at Goddard (i.e., create a "yellow pages" of expertise), and place this information online on either Goddard's intranet or its website to serve as a "know-who" directory.
- Continue to codify and centrally house Goddard's "explicit" knowledge through such projects as Goddard's Directory of Projects (library) and Knowledge Nuggets.
- Further develop NASA's Lessons Learned Information System (LLIS), and "push" appropriate lessons learned to individuals who could most benefit from them. Encourage the submission and use of lessons at Goddard (and throughout NASA) and use of the LLIS.
- Develop case studies of successful and unsuccessful Goddard missions, and make them available so learning can take place by others.
- Continue to create a knowledge preservation system using web-based, searchable video techniques to capture "war stories" from Goddard program and project managers.
- Provide an incentive reward structure to motivate employees to share knowledge.
- Continue to encourage involvement in the Goddard-wide formal mentoring program.
- Explore the development of the parameters of a "knowledge" performance factor that can eventually be incorporated into annual performance appraisals.

- Where appropriate, require that "lessons learned" be recorded during project development and implementation, before final sign-off can occur.
- Continue to encourage knowledge sharing in key competencies at informal get-togethers to facilitate the emergence of "communities of practice" that share knowledge on an ongoing basis (personalization approach).
- Access key experts who recently retired to capture their knowledge for permanent inclusion in the knowledge management system, and develop formalized methods and innovative ways to bring retirees back on a part-time basis. Exit interviews should also be considered to be part of this knowledge retention system.
- Encourage directors to present, on an ongoing basis, internal tutorials on hot topics (and capture and disseminate them on the intranet).
- Assign knowledge stewards in each directorate and knowledge retention managers on each project team.

KM TODAY

Sir Francis Bacon's adage "knowledge is power" is now being replaced by "Sharing knowledge is power." At least, this is the hope of the KM community. The ability to share knowledge must be a basic tenet of knowledge management if knowledge management is to survive. Knowledge management is the process of creating value from an organization's intangible assets (e.g., brainpower, intellectual property, and customer relationships). It deals with how best to leverage knowledge internally and externally (Liebowitz 1999, Liebowitz 2001). Building and nurturing a knowledge-sharing culture is the essence of knowledge management.

Organizations are engaging in knowledge management for a number of key reasons: to increase innovation and creativity; to leverage knowledge internally and externally for improved worker productivity and customer relations; to capture and preserve knowledge for building the organization's institutional memory; and to improve efficiency and effectiveness of decision making. If an organization is to be high performing, KM plays a crucial role in transforming the organization into a well-oiled, thriving business.

What does it mean to be high performing? Many analysts feel that an organization needs to adapt quickly to changes in the marketplace, and knowledge management offers a way to do this. According to George Lawton (2001), knowledge management's key technologies enable:

- content and workflow management, which categorize knowledge and direct it to workers who can benefit from it;

- search functionality, to let users look for relevant knowledge; and
- collaboration, to help workers share knowledge.

Through the use of intelligent agents (software programs that act autonomously without human intervention), knowledge management systems can push relevant lessons learned to individuals in the organization who can benefit from them in order to build the organizational intelligence of the firm. Data and text mining can also be used to develop user profiles to push relevant information and knowledge from repositories to employees and customers.

Technology can be used to facilitate knowledge sharing, but knowledge sharing is more about people and culture. Simply put, people have to be willing to share their knowledge in order for individual, group, and organizational learning to take place. According to a survey by International Data Corporation and *Knowledge Management* magazine in May 2001 (Chiem 2001), the second biggest implementation challenge for knowledge management (named by 36.6 percent of respondents) is that the current culture does not encourage sharing.

Sharing knowledge runs counter to what we have traditionally been taught. Throughout our formal education, we are usually assessed on individualized learning and what "I" know versus what "we" know. This promotes a "knowledge is power" attitude that seems ingrained in us starting early in life. Perhaps an interesting twist for encouraging a knowledge-sharing culture during our educational experience would be to define cheating as the failure to help someone in time of need. Thus, if you don't share your knowledge and experience when needed, then you may be guilty of cheating.

Stephen Denning, consultant and former director of knowledge management at the World Bank, indicates in his laws of knowledge management that knowledge is key to economic survival. Specifically, he states that knowledge sharing is increasingly seen as the sine qua non to survival. Denning indicates that organizations must develop a knowledge-sharing culture and knowledge-sharing processes (www.stephendenning.com). In this sense, knowledge sharing is not merely an alternative strategic option but is required for organizational survival.

A critical element of knowledge sharing is building trust. Phat Chiem (2001) indicates that trust supports the knowledge management process by giving people confidence to propose new ideas and by recognizing their contributions when these ideas succeed. A lack of trust, therefore, will promote a knowledge-hoarding culture instead of a knowledge-sharing one.

High-performing organizations generally have high organizational intelligence. I view organizational intelligence as the collective assemblage of all intelligences that contribute toward building a shared vision, a renewal process, and a direction for the entity (Liebowitz 2000). Organizational intelligence involves the following knowledge functions: transforming information into knowledge; identifying and verifying knowledge; capturing and securing knowledge; organizing knowledge; retrieving and applying knowledge; combining knowledge; creating knowledge; learning knowledge; and distributing or selling knowledge.

Knowledge exchange is crucial to promoting a high-performing organization, which is a basic tenet of knowledge management. In some interesting work on electronic communities of practice, McClure-Wasko and Faraj (2000) found that to increase knowledge exchange, organizations should consider using knowledge management systems that connect members to open-membership electronic communities of practice and should establish a cultural norm that encourages knowledge sharing by acknowledging the reputation and status of organizational members actively engaged in their electronic community. McClure-Wasko and Faraj found that extrinsic (rather than intrinsic) reward systems may not be the best approach for increasing knowledge exchange. Rather, successful communities have members that act out of community interest (intrinsic value) rather than self-interest, because extrinsic rewards promote self-interest. Increased knowledge exchange hopefully leads to increased knowledge flow and innovation within the community and organization.

Ryder System Inc., the transportation and logistics firm based in Miami, has developed a knowledge center. According to the March 2001 issue of *Knowledge Management* (www.destinationkm.com), the Ryder executives and others in the organization have embraced knowledge management, and the firm's knowledge center supports various internal communities and provides a way to produce better and quicker business proposals. This type of knowledge management helps to make Ryder a high-performing organization.

If an organization is to be adaptable, flexible, and innovative, knowledge management needs to be an essential part of the organization's strategy. In today's rapidly changing and competitive environment, high-performing organizations are the ones most likely to survive. Creating knowledge through knowledge management initiatives will help to produce high-performing organizations, and the double-loop learning effect should increase an organization's innovation and adaptability.

Knowledge management is becoming more pervasive in organizations as critical knowledge is being lost through attrition, early retirements, lack of infusion of new talent, and other reasons. According to Shereen Remez, the director of knowledge management at AARP (formerly the American Association for Retired Persons), about 80 percent of industry have knowledge management teams, and around 25 percent have chief knowledge officers or the equivalent (Eisenhart 2001). In government, around half of the federal civilian workforce is eligible to retire in the next few years. This shows that it is crucial to capture and share key knowledge before employees leave the organization. At NASA, for example, a strategic knowledge management team has been in existence for over five years, composed of representatives from the ten NASA centers and NASA headquarters.

A major difference between the public and private sectors that affects knowledge management's effectiveness is the recognition and reward structure. In the government, employees are typically evaluated on a pass-fail system as part of their annual performance plan. Additionally, monetary rewards are restricted in the government as compared to industry. Thus, providing a motivation and reward structure for knowledge sharing in the government is more challenging than in industry. Siemens, for example, gave away a Porsche 911 to employees who were willing to actively share their knowledge the most. Other organizations have given frequent-flier miles, gifts, monetary amounts, and other incentives to encourage knowledge sharing.

According to a study I coauthored (Montano, Buchwalter, and Liebowitz 2001), the practice of knowledge management in public and private organizations is very similar at the macro level, even though the reasons for undertaking KM initiatives differ. For example, both types of organizations have best-practice and lessons-learned repositories. Similarly, both types of organizations encourage knowledge sharing through incentives. The difference is in the types of incentives employed, which are influenced by work contexts. According to Shereen Remez, the U.S. government has no single, overarching KM strategy — agencies are learning through experimentation (Eisenhart 2001).

KM TOMORROW

Grover and Davenport (2001) suggest a pragmatic framework for KM research. They look at individual/work (emergent) knowledge management processes and organizational (deliberate) processes. Strategy, structure, culture, and information technology (IT) infrastructure impact these processes to generate knowledge management outcomes. Alavi and Leidner (2001) suggest a series of knowledge management research issues that center around knowledge creation, knowledge storage and retrieval, knowledge transfer, and knowledge application. The research questions include:

- What conditions facilitate knowledge creation in organizations?
- Do certain organizational cultures foster knowledge creation?

- Can IT enhance knowledge creation by enabling weak ties to develop and by reinforcing existing close ties?
- How is knowledge originating from outside a unit evaluated for internal use?
- Does lack of a shared context inhibit the adoption of knowledge originating from outside a unit?
- What incentives are effective in encouraging knowledge contribution and sharing in organizations?
- How much context needs to be included in knowledge storing to ensure effective interpretation and application?
- Is stored knowledge accessed and applied by individuals who do not know the originator of the knowledge?
- What retrieval mechanisms are most effective in enabling knowledge retrieval?
- How can knowledge be effectively transferred among organizational units?
- To what degree does the application of IT to knowledge transfer increase the transfer of knowledge among individuals within a group and between groups?
- What organizational and technical strategies are effective in facilitating knowledge transfer?
- What social, cultural, or technical attributes of organizational settings encourage knowledge transfer by balancing the push and pull processes?
- Does the application of IT to knowledge transfer inadvertently discourage external searches for knowledge?
- How can an organization encourage application of knowledge that is made available?
- What factors contribute to the knowing-doing gap in organizations and how can they be reduced or eliminated?
- What organizational practices can help bridge the knowledge application gap?

Other knowledge management research issues are:

- Developing "active" analysis and dissemination techniques for knowledge sharing and searching via intelligent agent technology
- Applying knowledge discovery techniques (data/text mining, neural networks, etc.) for mining knowledge bases or repositories
- Improving query capabilities through natural-language-understanding techniques
- Developing metrics for measuring value added by knowledge management
- Developing standardized methodologies for knowledge management development and knowledge audits

- Providing improved techniques for performing knowledge mapping and building knowledge taxonomies/ontologies
- Developing techniques for building collaborative knowledge bases
- Developing improved tools for capturing knowledge from various media (looking at multimedia mining to induce relationships among images, videos, graphics, text, etc.)
- Developing techniques for integrating databases to avoid "stovepiping" or functional silos
- Building improved software tools for developing and nurturing communities of practice
- Developing techniques for categorizing, synthesizing, and summarizing lessons learned (looking at text summarization techniques)
- Exploring ways to improve human-agent collaboration

Becerra-Fernandez and Sabherwal's work (2001) on organizational knowledge management at NASA's Kennedy Space Center found that combination and externalization processes, but not internalization and socialization processes, affect perceived knowledge satisfaction. Both of the knowledge management processes that provide explicit knowledge (i.e., combination processes, which help integrate several codified areas of knowledge, and externalization processes, which help explicate tacit knowledge) contribute to knowledge satisfaction. This finding is useful to organizations with an orientation toward science and engineering, but further studies should be conducted to replicate these results.

Fischer and Ostwald (2001) feel that ongoing collaborative knowledge construction and sharing are difficult processes. To make real progress with KM requires changing work practices, mind-sets, and reward structures.

Looking five to eight years ahead, what will be the key issues facing management and organizations? Hopefully, knowledge management will become woven into the fabric of organizations so that better techniques are used for capturing, sharing, and disseminating knowledge. Wireless computing will also become omnipresent and will continue to permeate corporate environments. Intelligent agent technology will certainly advance so that learning will take place automatically in these software agents. But what are the main dilemmas that management will face that will drive the need for improved solutions? As the workforce is graying, the loss of key expertise in organizations will continue to be a major problem in the foreseeable future. The need for adaptive, agile organizations to cope with the Internet and e-business world and the rapidly diminishing half-life of information will require organizations to be innovative in faster, cheaper, and improved ways. International competition will certainly increase and will push organizations to either partner strategically, as is being done today, or face the onslaught of competition from such growing, high-brain-power economies as Brazil, India, China, and others.

In order to foster innovation and agility, organizations in the coming years will continue to strive to be "learning organizations." Knowledge management will certainly contribute to the goal of knowledge creation and continuous learning. According to Reid Smith, vice president of knowledge management at Schlumberger, the new challenge for knowledge management will be reinventing the organization as a provider of products and services that are possible only because it is able to leverage the collective knowledge of its people (Smith and Farquhar 2000). To help in this regard, Hugh McKellar, the *KM World* executive editor, believes the next-generation portal will plug the best enterprise knowledge from all diverse divisions into the corporate bus, apply abstract/contextual reasoning to it, and automatically deliver it to the appropriate person or persons (www.kmworld.com). Artificial intelligence will play a major role in making these visions become reality.

A key element in creating learning organizations is transforming individualized learning into organizational learning. By building its collective intelligence, an organization can prosper through improved knowledge-sharing mechanisms. Text mining and other knowledge discovery techniques will also be useful in creating knowledge for organizational intelligence. Embedding knowledge management processes within the business processes of the organization should help the organization in its "learning and unlearning" cycles.

Smith and Farquhar (2000) look at the road ahead for knowledge management. They feel that the "knowledge-powered enterprise" should be the goal for the next stop on the road. In such an organization, knowledge management is "organic" in that it happens everywhere, and in real time. Knowledge management process and behavior are embedded in the workflow as part of daily job activities. KM functions are embedded in core business applications and employee productivity tools. Smith and Farquhar feel that the new focus is the end game for knowledge management—fostering knowledge creation and innovation by continuous learning to replenish and renew an organization's stocks of knowledge.

The years ahead look promising for organizations that put "learning" into their title. Knowledge management is putting us on the road to get there, but it's only a start.

REFERENCES

Alavi, M., and D. Leidner (2001), "Knowledge Management and Knowledge Management Systems: Conceptual Foundations and Research Issues," *MIS Quarterly*, Vol. 25, No. 1, Society for Information Management, March.

Becerra-Fernandez, I., and R. Sabherwal (2001), "Organizational Knowledge Management: A Contingency Perspective," *Journal of Management Information Systems*, Vol. 18, No. 1, M.E. Sharpe, Summer.

Chiem, P. (2001), "Trust Matters," *Knowledge Management*, Freedom Technology Media Group, May.

Eisenhart, M. (2001), "Washington's Need to Know," *Knowledge Management*, Freedom Technology Media Group, January.

Fischer, G., and J. Ostwald (2001), "Knowledge Management: Problems, Promises, Realities, and Challenges," *IEEE Intelligent Systems*, Vol. 16, No. 1, IEEE Computer Society Press, January/February.

Grover, V., and T. Davenport (2001), "General Perspectives on Knowledge Management: Fostering a Research Agenda," *Journal of Management Information Systems*, Vol. 18, No. 1, M.E. Sharpe, Summer.

Lawton, G. (2001), "Knowledge Management: Ready for Prime Time?" *Computer*, IEEE Computer Society Press, February.

Liebowitz, J. (2000), *Building Organizational Intelligence: A Knowledge Management Primer*, CRC Press, Boca Raton, Fla.

Liebowitz, J. (2001), *Knowledge Management: Learning from Knowledge Engineering*, CRC Press, Boca Raton, Fla.

Liebowitz, J. (ed.) (1999), *The Knowledge Management Handbook*, CRC Press, Boca Raton, Fla.

McClure-Wasko, M., and S. Faraj (2000), "It Is What One Does: Why People Participate and Help Others in Electronic Communities of Practice," *Journal of Strategic Information Systems*, Vol. 9, Elsevier.

Montano, B., J. Buchwalter, and J. Liebowitz (2001), "Knowledge Management in the Public Sector: A U.S. Social Security Administration Case Study," *Government Information Quarterly*, JAI Press.

Smith, R., and A. Farquhar (2000), "The Road Ahead for Knowledge Management: An AI Perspective," *AI Magazine*, Vol. 21, No. 4, AAAI Press, Winter.

Vestal, W. (2005), "Making Sense Out of KM Costs," *KMWorld*, July/August.

Chapter Three

KM in the Life of an Information and Library Professional

Knowledge management has been around for eons. The underlying concepts have existed for many years. Knowledge management draws from various fields and disciplines, including the library and information science disciplines. Even though some of the KM terms seem novel, many of the foundational elements behind it come from the library and information sciences. When we talk about ontologies, knowledge representation, knowledge preservation, codified sources, taxonomies, and the like, we can see that the library sciences have had profound, early impacts on the field of knowledge management.

In recent years, a number of library and information science programs have started degrees, certificates, and concentrations in knowledge management. Table 3.1 shows some sample programs in these areas.

Many librarians might be called knowledge managers. In Bryan Craig's article on LIScareer.com (the Library and Information Science Professional's Career Development Center, 2003), he states that librarians know about information and knowledge and how to manage them. Librarians have always examined how information is created, cataloged, stored, and retrieved. As far back as the 1998 International Federation of Library Associations and Institutions General Conference, Denis Reardon (1998) authored a paper titled "Knowledge Management: The Discipline for Information and Library Science Professionals." In this paper, he indicates that the areas of study for knowledge management overlap many of the library and information science techniques, skills, and methodologies. Such areas of study include information technology, electronic resources, communications technology, management, information management, research skills, transferable skills, knowledge studies, and behavioral studies.

Table 3.1.   Sample KM Programs Throughout the Library and Information Science Field

Institution	Program
University of Denver	MLIS with a KM Concentration, Certificate in KM
University of Oklahoma	MS in KM
University of Canberra	MS in KM (School of Information Management)
Curtin University of Technology	Graduate Certificate in KM
University of South Australia	Graduate Certificate in KM
Royal Roads University, Canada	MA, Graduate Diploma, Graduate Certificate in KM
University of Maryland, College Park	Master of Information Management
Johns Hopkins University (Business & Education)	Graduate Certificate in Competitive Intelligence
Simmons College	Graduate Certificate in Competitive Intelligence
George Washington University (Engineering Management)	MS and PhD in Knowledge Management
Kent State University	MS in Information Architecture and Knowledge Management
Nanyang Technological University, Singapore	MS in KM
Dominican University	MS in KM
California State University– Northridge	MS in KM

At a later IFLA General Conference, in August 2000, Tan Shanhong (2000) presented a paper titled "Knowledge Management in Libraries in the 21st Century." This paper discusses the evolving role of the library from the conventional functions of collecting, processing, disseminating, storing, and utilizing document information to the new knowledge-era roles of serving as a treasurehouse of human knowledge and participating in knowledge innovation activities. The Special Libraries Association, during this time, started an Institute for Knowledge Executives to educate library and information science professionals on the state of the art of knowledge management. Additionally, Michael Koenig and Kanti Srikantaiah edited two important books on knowledge management for library and information science professionals—*Knowledge Management for the Information Professional* (2000) and *Knowledge Management: Lessons Learned* (2004).

The role of library and information professionals in knowledge management was further evidenced by studies such as one by Isola Ajiferuke of the University of Western Ontario (2003) and others. Ajiferuke's study showed that 86 percent of the information professionals surveyed are involved in their organization's KM programs. The KM roles that these individuals play include designing the information architecture, developing taxonomies, managing content on the organization's intranet, collecting competitive intelligence, and providing research services to the KM team.

KNOWLEDGE MANAGEMENT CYCLE

Knowledge management typically involves four major functions: (1) knowledge identification and capture, (2) knowledge sharing, (3) knowledge application, and (4) knowledge creation. These four activities constitute the knowledge management life cycle. Once crucial "at risk" knowledge is identified, it is captured in some form—either codified or personalized. Then, the knowledge is shared with others and applied in a specific context. After the knowledge is internalized and combined with other knowledge that the knowledge recipient possesses, new insights develop (knowledge creation), and this "new" knowledge then is captured, shared, and applied, and the cycle continues.

Information and library science professionals have many roles to contribute to the knowledge management life cycle. A key KM role stemming from the cataloging function, where information and library professionals can assist, involves the creation of a knowledge taxonomy. This function also includes the creation of metadata standards in which a taxonomy is one part of a metadata scheme. The taxonomy can be used as the standardized lexicon for developing the content and document management systems, as well as the expertise locator system. Information professionals can help refine the search functions for locating important information and knowledge, and they can help find improved methods of disseminating information and knowledge. Additionally, the library professional has traditionally been involved in information capture and can apply similar techniques toward knowledge capture, retention, and preservation.

Information and library science professionals can also aid in the competitive intelligence (CI) function, an area related to knowledge management. As discussed in an earlier chapter, KM is similar to looking down your office hallway, and CI is like looking out your office window. The goal of CI is to systematically develop a way to collect, analyze, and manage external information for the purpose of improving organizational decision making. The library professional has been involved in primary and secondary research methods, which would naturally be applied in CI. About 50 percent of CI is still the collection effort—where information and library professionals can make a great impact. The CI analysis function can also be facilitated by knowledge from information and library professionals. Data and text mining techniques could be used by information and library professionals to better analyze structured and unstructured data and text to uncover hidden patterns and relationships.

Often, organizations initiate projects that could be considered "low-hanging fruit" (e.g., developing document management systems or online communities of practice) when it comes time to explore knowledge management. The conversation below is fairly typical in many organizations:

"I can't seem to find the right document or the right person to speak with!" Jill exclaims. "We have all these different versions of our financial, legal, and other reports and documents on our shared drive and on our own personal hard drives, which makes it difficult to quickly access the right information at the time we need it. Additionally, we use Lotus Notes at headquarters and Outlook/Exchange in the affiliates, and everyone prefers the look of their own system. We want to have a seamless integration process so we don't have to work in our e-mail system, and then go to the document management system, and then move to Word or Excel. We'd love to have a one-stop shopping system with native integration of software packages, as well as the capability to create, store, search, and retrieve documents in at least English, Spanish, and Russian. It would be great to be able to search on videos or webcasts that are part of the repository and have ways to automatically tag and dynamically develop the taxonomy for labeling and searching all types of documents and images. Having some visualization techniques to better display searches and clusters of documents and to help us navigate through the 150,000+ documents would be extremely helpful. Also, an ability to store lessons learned and best practices would be needed, and having capabilities to capture the tacit knowledge that we have would be very useful."

Jill takes a deep breath of air. "And that's only for the document management piece of our knowledge management solution," she points out. "We also want to develop online communities and expertise locator systems across our worldwide regions, hubs, affiliates, and headquarters, with about a thousand users. Of course, part of the challenge is the varying degree of Internet connectivity in some of these remote parts of the world—even using 28-baud hookups. The collaboration part of our KM approach could perhaps give us the most impact in terms of sharing information and knowledge across online communities, similar to what the World Bank and other organizations have used. But we thought we would start with the document management system component of our KM strategy as a low-hanging fruit."

A typical schedule for a demonstration project for a document management system pilot is shown below:

Document Management System (DMS) Pilot Schedule

May 1–7:
- Develop a short list of DMS vendors to come for a demo, based on draft functional requirements (determine the types and quantity of content to be housed in the DMS and what critical subset would be best for the DMS pilot)

May 8–14:
  • Invite three to four vendors to demo their DMS tools and respond to functional requirements

May 15:
  • Brief the KM committee

May 16–23:
  • Observe vendor demos
  • Receive vendor proposals
  • Finalize the subset of content to include for the DMS pilot version

May 24–30:
  • Evaluate proposals and select vendor
  • Procure DMS tool

June and July:
  • Load DMS tool on organization's system/network
  • Train IT staff on how to work the DMS tool
  • Develop taxonomy
  • Populate the content and customize the user interface in the DMS

August:
  • Train users on how to use the DMS
  • Test usability of the DMS in a test pilot
  • Analyze the user evaluation comments

September:
  • Incorporate the users' comments into the DMS
  • Expand the DMS content based on user feedback
  • Further train the users on the DMS worldwide
  • Show Version 1 of the DMS (end of September)

In selecting a document management system, various multiple-criteria decision-making approaches can be used. One popular technique is the Analytic Hierarchy Process developed by Thomas Saaty at the University of Pittsburgh. This technique uses paired comparisons to quantify subjective judgments used in decision making. A tree hierarchy is constructed in which the goal is positioned at the top, criteria and subcriteria are listed next, and alternatives are included at the lower part of the tree (www.expertchoice.com). In the example above, a software package, Expert Choice, was used to automate the Analytic Hierarchy Process. The possible alternatives included seven of the leading document management system/portal packages: SharePoint, Plumtree, Documentum, Autonomy, Livelink, Hummingbird, and Interwoven. The criteria included cost, document management capabilities, collaboration capabilities,

scalability. integration/migration, vendor support, and ease of use. The following
list shows the ranking of the criteria and alternatives after applying the Analytic
Hierarchy Process. Microsoft's SharePoint was ranked the best choice after the
results were synthesized. The 0.05 overall inconsistency index is tolerable, as it
should be 0.10 or less (i.e., the judgments were at least 90 percent consistent).

Cost = 0.265
  Autonomy = 0.017
  SharePoint = 0.136
  Plumtree = 0.018
  Interwoven = 0.021
  Hummingbird = 0.033
  Documentum = 0.013
  Livelink = 0.027
Document management capabilities = 0.252
  Autonomy = 0.066
  SharePoint = 0.014
  Plumtree = 0.014
  Interwoven = 0.021
  Hummingbird = 0.052
  Documentum = 0.052
  Livelink = 0.034
Collaboration capabilities = 0.172
  Autonomy = 0.009
  SharePoint = 0.041
  Plumtree = 0.056
  Interwoven = 0.009
  Hummingbird = 0.019
  Documentum = 0.010
  Livelink = 0.028
Scalability = 0.073
  Autonomy = 0.013
  SharePoint = 0.008
  Plumtree = 0.012
  Interwoven = 0.007
  Hummingbird = 0.011
  Documentum = 0.010
  Livelink = 0.011
Integration/migration = 0.088
  Autonomy = 0.014
  SharePoint = 0.005

    Plumtree = 0.014
    Interwoven = 0.014
    Hummingbird = 0.014
    Documentum = 0.014
    Livelink = 0.014
  Vendor support = 0.056
    Autonomy = 0.007
    SharePoint = 0.018
    Plumtree = 0.006
    Interwoven = 0.007
    Hummingbird = 0.007
    Documentum = 0.004
    Livelink = 0.007
  Ease of use = 0.094
    Autonomy = 0.023
    SharePoint = 0.014
    Plumtree = 0.014
    Interwoven = 0.005
    Hummingbird = 0.019
    Documentum = 0.005
    Livelink = 0.014

Overall inconsistency index = 0.05
    Autonomy = 0.149
    SharePoint = 0.236
    Plumtree = 0.134
    Interwoven = 0.085
    Hummingbird = 0.155
    Documentum = 0.107
    Livelink = 0.134

TOTAL: 1.000

KNOWLEDGE MANAGEMENT FOR THE
INFORMATION AND LIBRARY PROFESSIONAL

Thus far in this chapter, we have discussed how information and library professionals can contribute toward the development of knowledge management systems in an organization. However, knowledge management can also play a vital role to make life easier for the information professional. Let's explore some possibilities.

Cataloging is a key function often associated with library professionals. In the past, cataloging has been an arduous task, but knowledge management and intelligent systems technology can be used to greatly ease this function. For example, the use of expert systems and intelligent agents can be applied to facilitate the cataloging function. As explained in a chapter I coauthored (Liebowitz and Adya 2000), intelligent agents could be used in digital library initiatives in the areas of filtering, retrieval, navigation, monitoring, recommending, and profiling. Expert systems might be used to help codify the rules of thumb for cataloging. Some knowledge management software, such as Autonomy, builds a dynamic taxonomy through probabilistic reasoning (using Bayes' theorem) so that cataloging and searching functions can be performed more easily by the information professional and the end user.

Searching is an active area of research in knowledge management, and advanced techniques dealing with clustering, data and text mining, neural networks, self-organizing maps, and other algorithmic approaches are being applied in order to improve search capabilities in knowledge management systems. This will ultimately afford information and library professionals greater ease in locating key documents, information, and knowledge for themselves and their customers.

Lessons-learned systems, online communities, and expertise locator systems will also enhance the role and value of the library and information professional. Capturing lessons learned and best practices relating to library functions can provide a rich source of information to help the information professional better perform his or her duties. Reaching out to various communities of peers through online communities can provide a ready source of knowledge to tap. Likewise, an expertise locator system can help the information professional quickly identify the right person for a set of questions.

Certainly, there is a symbiotic relationship between information and library professionals and knowledge management. Information and library professionals can contribute greatly to the advancement of knowledge management, and knowledge management can also advance the role and capabilities of information and library professionals. In the next section, we will explore the changing role of information and library professionals in a knowledge management context.

HOW KNOWLEDGE MANAGEMENT TRANSFORMS THE ROLE OF INFORMATION AND LIBRARY PROFESSIONALS

In order for library and information professionals to fully utilize the merits of knowledge management, the roles and responsibilities of the library will have to change. Today's library has gradually been transformed over the years. The university library, for example, has become a social meeting place in addition to its traditional role as a place to study, research, and locate information. Part of this transformation is due to the wealth of electronic resources, many of which can be accessed from the home or dormitory. Coffee bars, lounges, and meeting rooms are now the norms in most university libraries, in addition to the usual stacks and study desks.

The organizational library can serve as the knowledge management branch for some organizations. Instead of a technocentric approach to KM, such as the IT department would take, or a human-centered approach, such as the human resources department would take, the library can offer a middle-of-the-road approach to KM. The library often includes specialists in information technology, information retrieval, knowledge preservation, and research services. The library can serve a brokering role in coordinating these specialists' expertise with that of the human resources, communications, public affairs, strategy, and IT departments and the business units in the organization. The library has always been a treasure-house of information, and it needs to continue to expand into the knowledge chest as well. The library could play a coordinator's role in integrating these other departments toward developing a KM presence in the organization.

This could be a workable situation, as no one will feel threatened by the library and the library connotes a fairly unbiased view, although the codification approach may be favored over the personalization approach due to the library's orientation. If the library takes an open perspective to matching the KM strategy to the organization's culture, the library can be successful in shepherding KM in the organization. Of course, many people view the library as a peripheral unit rather than as a central department in the organization. This could create credibility problems, as KM needs to be a critical strategy infused throughout the entire organization. A KM champion within the senior leadership will need to be identified to work with the library and the KM team for financial and moral support.

In my article "A Knowledge Management Implementation Plan at a Leading U.S. Technical Government Organization: A Case Study" (Liebowitz 2003), I discuss various role changes in a government organization that were needed for knowledge management to become a workable strategy. The following are examples of knowledge management roles suggested for NASA's Goddard Space Flight Center:

Library: acts as the central repository for knowledge and record preservation, as well as developing, together with the information systems group, and maintaining the web-based, multimedia asset management system; works with intranet/web colleagues to develop taxonomies; works with the public affairs department in "pushing" relevant articles of interest to staff, general public, and key stakeholders; assists employees in their research.

TV studios: hold knowledge-capture sessions.

Public affairs department: facilitates the dissemination of internal and external knowledge-sharing efforts.

Information systems group: handles the development and maintenance of the intranet, website, lessons-learned system, and expertise directory, as well as managing, together with the library, the development of the web-based, searchable multimedia asset management system.

Engineering directorate: coordinates, along with the knowledge management officer, the development and offering of organization-wide mini-courses in selected critical knowledge areas.

Human resources department: promotes learning and knowledge-sharing proficiencies as part of the recognition and reward system and possibly the annual performance development plan; assists knowledge stewards, if necessary, in exit interviews; manages the mentoring program.

All directorates: assign respected individuals to act as facilitators of online communities of practice; continue informal knowledge-sharing sessions (brown-bag lunches, "learn and lunch" sessions, knowledge fairs, etc.).

Besides these roles, someone typically oversees the knowledge management initiatives in the organization. This individual usually holds the title of chief knowledge officer, knowledge management officer, knowledge management architect, knowledge management director, director of intellectual capital, chief learning officer, or the like. This KM leader usually has a background in one or more of the following areas: information and library sciences, human resources, organizational development, strategy, business development, research and development, marketing, and finance. In the U.S. government, many of the KM responsibilities are being subsumed within a larger context—strategic human capital. In this manner, the chief human capital officer may ultimately oversee the KM efforts as part of his or her charter. The KM leader usually has a KM team consisting of representatives from the major departments or divisions in the organization and from human resources, the library, IT, public affairs, communications, strategy, and other interested parties.

SUMMARY

As discussed in this chapter, information and library professionals have an integral role to play with respect to knowledge management. The library should take a more active role in shaping the knowledge management strategy and initiatives in the organization. Similar to the way that many lessons-learned systems are ineffective due to passive analysis and dissemination of lessons learned, the library could suffer the same fate if it becomes complacent and doesn't seize the opportunities that KM can offer.

In addition, KM can enhance the daily work activities of the information and library professional, and traditional functions in the organization can be reshaped by KM roles and responsibilities. In the future, KM will be more pervasive and transparent in the organization as it becomes embedded in the daily activities of the employees.

REFERENCES

Ajiferuke, I. (2003), "Role of Information Professionals in Knowledge Management Programs: Empirical Evidence from Canada," *Informing Science Journal*, Vol. 6, http://inform.nu.

Craig, B. (2003), "Wanted: Chief Knowledge Officers," LIScareer.com (the Library and Information Science Professional's Career Development Center), November.

Koenig, M., and K. Srikantaiah (eds.) (2000), *Knowledge Management for the Information Professional*, American Society for Information Science, Silver Spring, Md.

Koenig, M., and K. Srikantaiah (eds.) (2004), *Knowledge Management: Lessons Learned*, American Society for Information Science, Silver Spring, Md.

Liebowitz, J. (2003), "A Knowledge Management Implementation Plan at a Leading U.S. Technical Government Organization: A Case Study," *Knowledge and Process Management Journal*, Vol. 10, No. 4, Wiley.

Liebowitz, J., and M. Adya (2000), "An Analysis of Using Expert Systems and Intelligent Agents for the Virtual Library Project at the Naval Surface Warfare Center–Carderock Division," in *World Libraries on the Information Superhighway*, Patricia Fletcher and John Bertot, eds., Idea Group Publishing, Hershey, Pa.

Reardon, D. (1998), "Knowledge Management: The Discipline for Information and Library Science Professionals," paper presented at the International Federation of Library Associations and Institutions General Conference, Amsterdam, August.

Shanhong, T. (2000), "Knowledge Management in Libraries in the 21st Century," paper presented at the International Federation of Library Associations and Institutions General Conference, Jerusalem, August.

Chapter Four

Is KM Right for You?

After reading this book so far, you may think that everyone should be engaged in knowledge management. Knowledge sharing is a form of collaboration and communication, and it can lead to new discoveries. However, for many reasons, many organizations feel that they aren't quite ready to embark on their KM journey. First, some organizations may inherently have a knowledge-hoarding culture versus a knowledge-sharing one. This type of culture could have grown over the many years of existence of a particular organization, and it could take years to break down the walls of these functional silos. Second, senior leaders may feel that KM is too long-term oriented and that they need short-term gains to survive in today's competitive environment. Thus, deciding not to put a large sum of money into KM and placing the dollars in something that seems more tangible and near-term is a common thought of many senior managers. Third, there may be those who think KM is a passing fad. They may not see the real value of KM to their organizations. Fourth, the organizations may not have the leadership and vision to see how KM can add value to the organization. Last, some organizations may not have the necessary resources—either financial or human—to make KM a reality.

So, how can you know whether KM is right for you? Over the years, I have developed a quick litmus test to see if an organization needs KM. Here it is:

- Is the average age of your employees fairly senior?
- Has your organization done a poor job of documenting processes and capturing knowledge?
- Do your competitors seem to be ahead of you by being engaged in KM efforts?

- Does your organization not have a formal mentoring program to help share and transfer knowledge between the experts and novices (newcomers) in the organization?
- Has little funding been put into employee training and development?
- Does one part of the organization typically not know what the other parts are doing, especially if working in a similar domain?
- Do you spend a good part of the day looking for information that has been misplaced?
- Do you feel that you don't have time to chat with your colleagues in the organization in an informal way?
- Are many of your knowledgeable employees leaving the organization through early buyouts, better job offers, or for other reasons?

If you can answer "yes" to seven to nine of the questions above, then your organization is in dire need of knowledge management. If you answer "yes" to four to six of the questions, then your organization can benefit from knowledge management. If you answer positively to three or fewer questions, then knowledge management might be helpful but probably will have less impact on your organization than on others.

In my experience, some organizations may feel that knowledge management is important but lack the necessary success factors for making KM beneficial to the organization. William Taylor and Greg Wright (2004) discuss the key successful factors for effective knowledge sharing: an open leadership climate, a capacity to learn from failure, good information quality, satisfaction with change processes, performance orientation, and a vision for change. An open leadership climate connotes an element of interpersonal trust in the organization. Learning from failure is also essential for developing a continuous learning culture in the organization. Management and employees should feel strongly that learning is a part of everyday work life.

There are numerous reasons why organizations adopt KM. From a 2002 survey on KM adoption compiled by International Data Corporation (IDC), the top reasons why organizations adopted knowledge management are, in order (http://www.destinationcrm.com/km/dcrm_km_article.asp?id=822):

1. Collaboration
2. Sharing best practices
3. E-learning
4. Customer relationship management
5. Project workspace
6. Competitive intelligence
7. Web publishing

8. Business processes
9. Supply chain management
10. Other

CAN KM ADVANCE YOUR CAREER AS AN INFORMATION AND LIBRARY PROFESSIONAL?

Knowledge management can open the horizons for information and library professionals. Even though some organizations may not have a formal KM program for one reason or another, most top managers agree that the knowledge of their employees provides the organization's competitive edge. As such, many senior leaders understand the value of KM and the benefits it offers for retaining, creating, and leveraging knowledge internally and externally. If the general notion of KM is understood by senior management, incorporating KM into one's working activities can be of great benefit. Thus, it would be worthwhile for information and library professionals to incorporate KM activities into their work lives.

There are many opportunities for information and library professionals to extend their expertise in the knowledge management field. The following are some recent KM-related job announcements (slightly modified from postings on www.tfpl.com), where you can see how a background in information and library sciences can come into play:

Job 1: An Information Services Manager is required by a leading law firm to take responsibility for the day-to-day operations of the Information Service. The role will involve management of staff; assisting the National Information Manager in the strategic development of the department; providing a full research and inquiry service; updating and maintenance of intranet pages; and the production and dissemination of current awareness bulletins as required by the business. A degree in Librarianship or Information Management, along with previous work experience in a commercial environment, is essential. You will need to have up-to-date knowledge of electronic products, including the Internet and intranets, and possess excellent communication skills. Knowledge of the legal sector is desirable.

Job 2: An international law firm requires a Program Manager (Knowledge Manager) to take the lead in the review and coordination of practice, product, and sector group KM plans. The role will involve coordination of the group's contributions to the intranet, including structural review of content; identifying knowledge needs; working on the development of a portal; and helping to establish communities of practice. You will need to be a graduate with at least five years' previous information and knowledge management experience within the professional services sector. Project management experience, strong communication skills, and teamwork skills are essential, as is an in-depth understanding of knowledge management. Knowledge of the legal sector is desirable.

Job 3: A Knowledge Manager is required to develop, promote, and implement knowledge management principles and practices for a large government agency. You will ensure that relevant expertise and learning experience is captured and made available through electronic and/or other means. You will undertake a knowledge audit to identify explicit and tacit knowledge to create a knowledge-sharing culture and improve the agency's learning environment. You will have substantial experience in an information and/or knowledge management role and of project management within tight time scales and resources. Up-to-date knowledge of theory and practice of knowledge capture, KM systems, and taxonomy is essential.

Job 4: Taxonomy/KM Analyst required to work on the trading floor of this leading international bank. You will be required to manage and support the Research Publishing and Taxonomy systems within the Fixed Income division. Managing the Fixed Income Taxonomy on a day-to-day basis, you will promote the role of taxonomy and maintain and seek to improve the use of content management technologies and methods. You will have strong communication skills to encourage better use of the research publishing tools and taxonomy. Knowledge of investment banking is essential, as is knowledge of training, taxonomy, and investment banking research, preferably fixed income.

CASE STUDY: DETERMINING THE
KM FIT FOR AN ORGANIZATION

In determining whether KM is appropriate for an organization, a knowledge audit is usually conducted first. The knowledge audit is a systematic review of the knowledge flows in the organization, and it assesses the types of KM approaches that would be of most benefit to the organization. It also contributes toward establishing a KM strategy for the organization. The following case study discusses a real situation in which a knowledge audit was conducted. For anonymity, I will use ORG as the name of the organization.

The Knowledge Audit Process at ORG

After reviewing various knowledge audit surveys, and using my own experience, I developed a knowledge audit survey instrument for ORG via iterations and successive refinements with the ORG management and staff. Appendix

A shows a version of the Knowledge Audit Questionnaire. A web-based version of the survey was used with SurveyMonkey. I received a 74 percent response rate with 53 surveys completed out of 72. The responses included a representative sample across departments and countries, as well as a representative sample of employees' length of time at ORG. Some of the employees who completed the survey (29.6 percent) had been a full-time employee at ORG for one to three years and were from a representative set of departments, regions, and countries. The following sections will analyze the key findings from the knowledge audit.

Knowledge Resources

The survey results indicated that 57.4 percent of employees preferred to e-mail or talk with an ORG colleague as their first choice in looking for information. The second course of action was to e-mail or talk to a colleague who works outside the organization. Performing a global web search, typically using Google, was also cited as a favored approach for looking for information. This suggests two key findings. First, ORG staff prefer the personalization approach—that is, people-to-people connections. This was further evidenced by the fact that the largest percentages of respondents indicated that they seek informal help from their immediate supervisor, a technical or functional expert, a peer or colleague in their department or country, and a peer or colleague outside their department or country, all on a weekly basis (43 percent, 43 percent, 45 percent, and 35 percent, respectively). Encouraging personalization approaches through knowledge-sharing forums, storytelling at staff meetings, brown-bag lunches, shadowing, mentoring, cross-functional teams, and face-to-face and online communities should be part of ORG's knowledge management strategy.

One interesting finding was that the department head (if different from the immediate supervisor) had the highest percentage (33 percent) associated with "never" being used as a source of help. ORG may want to look closely at the reasons for this occurrence and try to develop closer relationships between department heads and employees. It may be that ORG is a relatively flat organization with the immediate supervisors serving as the department heads. If this were the case, it would explain the occurrence above.

Another interesting finding from the survey was that top experts were infrequently accessed for help. Follow-up interviews with the ORG staff should be conducted to further validate this result.

In terms of the resources that people typically used to perform their job, e-mail was the predominant response (88 percent). E-mail was the bloodstream of the organization, especially for communicating to the various hubs abroad.

As for codified sources of information that ORG staff access and apply to do their jobs, ORG staff actively apply their own database and personal contact list files (73 percent) on a daily basis, as well as accessing their own notes or procedures (49 percent) on a daily basis. Use of the organization's intranet on a weekly basis for help in doing one's job was cited by 25 percent of the respondents, and 25 percent said that they never used it. This suggested that the existing databases, websites, and intranet were not providing the full capability that staff members needed and that it would be wise to include employee "cheat sheets" on the intranet and in a document management system. A challenge existed here for ORG to further develop the intranet by enriching it as a resource (i.e., incorporating a document management system or other relevant resources previously mentioned) so that it would be used on a daily basis.

Another interesting finding regarding knowledge resources is that the ORG department, division, and vendor procedure manuals were rarely used. ORG and department-specific policy manuals were used by only 29 percent of respondents on a quarterly basis. Likewise, department or division-operated databases (such as a shared calendar) were never used by 43 percent of the respondents.

Who did ORG employees seek out for work-related advice? The top individuals cited were A. S. (6 times), S. G. (5 times), and G. A. (4 times). This suggested that ORG should consider these individuals as points of knowledge and try to leverage their knowledge throughout the organization. This could be accomplished by pairing them with up-and-coming project leaders, having them give tutorials in their areas of expertise to the organization's employees, and developing a strategy and method to capture their expertise for knowledge-retention purposes.

Knowledge Sharing and Use

The survey responses for knowledge use indicated that the ORG staff members typically use data or information that one has to retrieve from a known source for answering a specific question (94.1 percent). After a task was completed, generating a written document, ORG staff members tended to save the document in an electronic file in their personal directory (66.7 percent), share/distribute it to others (60.8 percent), or save it on a shared directory (58.8 percent). In addition, many staff members also saved the document in a personal paper file (47.1 percent).

When asked about sharing information or an announcement that could be useful to other ORG staff, most respondents (56 percent) indicated that they would tell them about it or distribute a copy to them personally. The numbers above indicated some encouraging news about a knowledge-sharing culture at ORG. In order for knowledge management to work, a knowledge-sharing culture (as opposed to a knowledge-hoarding environment) is a key component for success. Continuing to build and nurture this knowledge-sharing culture is crucial for ORG to meet its strategic goals. ORG should consider including learning and knowledge-sharing proficiencies as part of the recognition and reward system in ORG. Building trust is also a central part of knowledge sharing. Some evidence from the open-ended questions, however, indicated that some interdepartmental distrust of colleagues, guarding of contacts too closely, and a department-ownership viewpoint may have inhibited the existence of an open knowledge-sharing culture at ORG.

The respondents indicated that the main constraints to sharing knowledge were mainly availability of time, lack of a well-organized central internal repository (i.e., the intranet) that is regularly updated and accessed by all staff, lack of knowledge about whom to go to for information and where the information exists (if at all), and poor Internet connections in some locations. The intranet should be developed to include a proper taxonomy for content and document management and should also include a "yellow pages" locator of ORG staff members and external experts. ORG should also have a library, with a library specialist.

The responses emphasized the need to apply best practices and lessons learned to ORG's internal and external activities. ORG's Virtual Best Practices Center is similar to a lessons-learned system (see NASA's Lessons Learned Information System at llis.nasa.gov). The lessons-learned or best-practice system should include a "push" approach (versus a "pull" approach) to send appropriate lessons to staff members at the time they need it, in order to push information about loans and grants, news updates, and other relevant information to ORG staff.

In terms of critical knowledge at risk of being lost because of turnover or lack of backup expertise, there appear to be several potential gaps. Some of these include ORG's "institutional memory" and historical knowledge base, documented decision rationales, relationship history with loan recipients and grantees, and other areas. Preserving and documenting the institutional knowledge of ORG would greatly help those in the future to not reinvent the wheel.

Training/Tools and Knowledge Needs

Echoing the "personalization" theme that pervaded the survey responses, most ORG staff (64.7 percent) preferred to get formal face-to-face training outside the workplace to learn or improve a skill, or have a friend or colleague show them how to do it (64.7 percent). Likewise, most staff members (88 percent) preferred to speak with a person in real time to help them do their job. Training on the "ORG basics" and having online training modules that could be accessed easily as refreshers might be useful for ORG. A strong need to be better informed on ORG-wide activities was evident from the surveys. A shared calendar with all ORG and related meetings (and deadlines) should be posted on the intranet, as well as summary reports. If such a calendar existed, perhaps ORG employees would use a shared calendar even though they haven't done so in the past. In terms of making knowledge available, survey respondents agreed (37 percent) that there was no easy way to make their knowledge available to others in ORG. These numbers suggest that people in ORG felt they had knowledge that could help others in ORG but didn't know the best mechanisms to share what they know with their colleagues. To address this concern, in addition to creating the previously mentioned "yellow pages" directory of experts on the intranet, ORG may want to think about having all-hands ORG-wide tutorials, instituting "hot topics" talks, using the intranet for posting lessons learned, and having online communities. The intranet should also have access to ORG PowerPoint slides, conference summaries, and other internal information. Agreement ranged from 45 to 55 percent that ORG employees would benefit from having templates, processes, and support to better share and document what they know.

In terms of the key items that should be included in ORG's document management system, the top recurring items were best practices, policies and procedures, forms, templates, and specific financial data. The highest-priority items (not in order) to include in the document management system were listed as:

- Legal documents
- Specific policies and procedures
- Industry best practices
- Who's who directory (name, title, function, responsibility)
- Grant data
- Expense report policies and procedures
- Training best practices
- Data warehousing of social and financial performance data
- HQ financial and operational data
- Product knowledge
- Forms
- Regulations
- Manual for ORG's operating system

- Country program profiles and related information
- Historical data
- Policy and organizational manuals
- Templates

Knowledge Flow

In terms of knowledge flow in the organization, respondents indicated how the knowledge flow in their area of responsibility could be improved. There were a myriad of responses, but several people agreed on these key areas: the need to have better access to information from other departments and the need to improve the communications flow among ORG locations worldwide. Many of the comments centered on improving the communications flow within and between groups. Instituting cross-functional teams should help to improve the communications flow in ORG. Also, the intranet should serve as a central repository for meeting summaries, calendars, and the like.

When asked about the mission-critical or operation-critical knowledge that they felt they possessed, ORG staff members gave many unique answers. Everyone seemed to feel that he or she had a strong contribution to make in a certain area of expertise. The main recurring responses were best practices of high-performing organizations and policy development. Since several people have experience in knowing best practices to be used in ORG, the best-practice/lessons-learned system should tap the expertise of these individuals to include their knowledge in the system.

Overall, the additional comments provided in the survey indicated that the staff members were pleased to participate in the knowledge audit and felt that it helped clarify their own role in ORG.

Specific Key Knowledge Management Recommendations for ORG to Undertake

A year after embarking on its formal knowledge management journey, ORG was (appropriately) looking inwardly for ways to best capture, share, and apply knowledge internally among its staff. As such, I recommended that ORG consider a number of key goals and initiatives as part of its knowledge management strategy:

Develop the organizational infrastructure to support knowledge management in ORG. This includes having designated knowledge coordinators to help populate content on the intranet and on the website, adding learning and knowledge-sharing proficiencies to the recognition and reward system at ORG in order to emphasize and reward people for sharing knowledge, and embedding knowledge management activities as part of everyone's daily work activities (e.g., capturing and using lessons learned and best practices during each project's life cycle, having relevant storytelling for the first five to ten minutes of staff meetings, and having after-action reviews at the end of each project). Processes should also be established for capturing knowledge, such as having knowledge elicitation sessions with a knowledge engineer, posting weekly reports on the intranet and categorizing or indexing them by subject, writing down lessons learned on a weekly or monthly basis for sharing at staff meetings and posting on the intranet, and holding exit interviews.

Develop the technology infrastructure (i.e., the intranet) to enable knowledge sharing to take place, and develop quick-win pilot projects. The intranet needed to be further developed within ORG, and appropriate resources should be allocated to ensure its development, content organization, nurturing, and maintenance (e.g., the IT staff should be actively involved in the intranet's development, and a library specialist, in addition to helping to create a library for ORG, should join the IT staff to help develop the taxonomy to be used for content, document, and knowledge management purposes on the intranet). As mentioned above, a calendar with all ORG and related meetings (and deadlines) should be posted on the intranet, along with online modules and "cheat sheets" for ORG training and instructions on how to perform various operations within ORG. List of internal frequently asked questions and responses, synopses of ORG and external reports, Excel and Word forms developed internally, local and national newspaper websites, and news clips should also be included on the intranet. The Google search engine should be included as part of the intranet for both internal and web searches. The intranet should also have links to three *essential* new projects: the "yellow pages" internal and external locator system, a document management system, and a best-practice/lessons-learned system (a virtual best-practice center). The "yellow pages" should include organizational responsibilities and subject-matter expertise. SharePoint, Livelink, Plumtree, Documentum, Autonomy, Interwoven, and Hummingbird should be considered as possible document management system/portal tools. The lessons-learned system should include a "push" feature to push appropriate new lessons to program staff and the external community who could benefit from these lessons. Since several staff members had experience in knowing best practices to be used in ORG, the best-practice/lessons-learned system should tap the expertise of these individuals. The "yellow pages" project should use software like AskMe (by AskMe Corporation) or Kamoon Connect to help create the directory. A longer-term project that should be undertaken by ORG is a web-based, searchable Knowledge Preservation Project to capture the institutional knowledge of experts in ORG and the rationale and decision-making processes behind certain decisions. Additionally, a process and a system to capture, analyze, interpret, and mine grant outcomes to inform ORG strategies should also be established.

Accentuate the "personalization" approach to knowledge sharing within ORG. A major part of this approach is to improve the flow of internal communications between departments, countries, regions, and hubs. Online communities of practice should be formed, with appropriate facilitators, to encourage knowledge sharing across ORG worldwide. Cross-functional teams should also be encouraged, which will enable people-to-people networking, allow connections to be made outside of one's own community or department, and integrate knowledge across functional silos. Meeting summaries, conference and trip reports, PowerPoint slides, and the like should be put on the intranet. Knowledge-sharing forums between experienced staff and those who are newer to ORG should be conducted, as well as brown-bag "Learn and Lunch" get-togethers. The Friday Reader is a wonderful mechanism to share information and knowledge at ORG. Since grant and loan management is a core competency of ORG, this was identified as a ripe area to target for such knowledge exchanges. A formal mentoring program should exist within ORG, and this will also help in improving communications flow within ORG, building and nurturing a knowledge-sharing culture, and increasing trust and a sense of belonging in ORG. Additionally, improved communications flow needs to exist throughout ORG, especially to the younger employees. Ways to make this improvement possible, besides a formal mentoring program, include having "open" meetings (such as strategy meetings and weekly team leader meetings) in order to keep everyone (especially the younger employees) better informed, and capturing and posting the minutes or summaries of these key meetings on the intranet.

Develop an external approach to knowledge management to share knowledge with ORG's loan recipients, grantees, customers, and stakeholders. ORG should concentrate on developing online communities of practice (similar to the World Bank's thematic groups) in order to encourage worldwide informal knowledge sharing among its hubs, regions, and loan recipients. Online communities have been a very successful knowledge management strategy and are used by many organizations (including the Fannie Mae Foundation, Best Buy, Hallmark, the Federal Aviation Administration, and NASA). ORG should pilot a few online communities with assigned facilitators or moderators, to see how things progress.

If ORG incorporates these recommendations for developing its knowledge management strategy and implementation plan, it will be on its way to successfully applying knowledge-sharing activities that will transform ORG into a "learning organization" and improve communications and effectiveness internally and externally.

REFERENCE

Taylor, W., and G. Wright (2004), "Organizational Readiness for Successful Knowledge Sharing: Challenges for Public Sector Managers," *Information Resources Management Journal*, Vol. 17, No. 2, Idea Group Publishing, April–June.

Chapter Five

Content, Document, Expertise, and Knowledge Management

What Should I Do First?

As organizations embark on knowledge management initiatives, it may be difficult to determine what project would give the organization the "greatest bang for the buck." Jim McKeen, Mike Zack, and Satyendra Singh's research (2005) certainly suggests that knowledge management leads to organizational and financial performance. Thus, it becomes readily apparent that knowledge management can add great value to an organization. But it is less clear what are the "low-hanging fruit" for developing initial KM projects for an organization. Should we first develop a content management system, a document management system, an expertise management system, a best-practice system, online communities, knowledge-sharing forums, or other types of knowledge management efforts?

Part of knowing what to do first will depend on the outcome of the knowledge audit, as discussed in the previous chapter. The knowledge audit will give a sense of the organizational culture and climate that will help to best match a KM approach and project with the organization's needs and culture. For example, if the organization leans toward codification approaches to KM rather than personalization techniques, this may suggest that the development of a KM system would be a mutually beneficial technique, given the organization's requirements and financial resources. However, if the organization prefers a "connection" approach versus a "collection" approach, then the use of online communities, knowledge fairs, brown-bag lunches, mentoring programs, job shadowing, job rotation, and knowledge-sharing forums may be a good match for first implementing knowledge management.

CONTENT MANAGEMENT SYSTEMS

Let's look at some of the favorite KM projects to gain an appreciation for which ones to use in an organization. According to the free encyclopedia Wikipedia (en.wikipedia.org), a content management system (CMS) is a "system used for organizing and facilitating collaborative creation of documents and other content." Content management systems are often web-based and allow online authoring, change approval, WYSIWYG (What You See Is What You Get) editing, workflow management, session and user management, indexing and searching, object storage, templating, and image and URL management.

Most organizations now refer to Enterprise Content Management (ECM) systems. According to AIIM (www.aiim.org), the worldwide association for ECM, Enterprise Content Management is "the technologies used to Capture, Manage, Store, Preserve, and Deliver content and documents related to organizational processes" (2006 definition from Wikipedia). Both ECM and CMS connote web content management, as well as multimedia/digital asset management. According to the Gartner Group, by 2008, 75 percent of Global 2000 companies will have a desktop-focused and a process-focused content management implementation (www.gartnergroup .com). Examples of ECMs are Interwoven (www.interwoven.com), Hummingbird (www.hummingbird.com), Documentum (www.documentum .com), and Livelink (www.opentext.com).

DOCUMENT MANAGEMENT SYSTEMS

Document management systems (DMSs) control documents from their creation through long-term archiving and typically include check-in/check-out, version management, search and navigation, and visualization functions. Electronic document management systems usually include a workflow model and digital rights management controls. According to Wikipedia, today's electronic document management is a key component of the broader framework of ECM. Over the recent years, content and document management systems have essentially been incorporated into ECM systems, along with portal capabilities.

A set of content/document management system requirements is shown as an example in table 5.1. These modified requirements were developed for a capstone project by MS-ITS students in a course I taught at Johns Hopkins University in spring 2005.

Table 5.1. Functional Requirements for a Content or Document Management System Portal

Req. #	Content Management Repository
1	The portal shall have the capability to share files among authorized users.
2	The portal shall allow users to view authorized files.
3	The portal shall allow authorized users to save files.
4	The portal shall allow authorized users to print files.
5	The portal shall allow users to e-mail files to other users in Microsoft Outlook.
6	The portal shall enable authorized users to download files.
7	The portal shall enable authorized users to upload files.
8	The portal shall allow authorized users to submit the following forms electronically.
9	The portal shall have the capability to create levels of hierarchy such as a home page, departmental page, and personal page.
10	The portal shall have the capability to allow authorized users based on security rights to customize the portal at any hierarchy level.
11	The portal shall have the capability to create an index of file directories.
12	The portal shall allow authorized users to create public and private folders.
13	The portal shall have the capability to support file documents in multiple file formats.
14	The portal shall have the capability to automatically create links to the files for user access.
15	The portal shall have the capability to display a list of files recently accessed by the user.
16	The portal shall support Digital Rights Management (DRM).
17	The portal shall have the capability to use the Windows cut and paste functionality.
18	The portal shall have the capability to integrate with standard Microsoft products.
19	The portal shall support the organization's standard publishing template.
20	The portal shall follow the organization's standard retention program for archiving and backing up files.
21	The portal shall support the ability to remove outdated documents by authorized individuals.
22	The portal shall have remote access capability.
23	The portal shall have the capability to route nonsignature forms electronically.
24	The portal shall allow documents to be stored as current or archived.

Req. #	Content Management System Document Version Control
25	The portal shall provide document version control.
26	The portal shall allow authorized users to check in a file under document version control.
27	The portal shall store an activity log associated with the document version control for each file.
28	The portal activity log shall display user name, check-in and check-out activity, and date-time stamp.

(continued)

Table 5.1. (*continued*)

Req. #	Content Management System Document Version Control
29	The portal shall display an activity log associated with the document version control for each file.

Req. #	Content Management System Applications Integration
30	The portal shall integrate with ORG's financial and accounting application software.
31	The portal shall integrate with ORG's HR software application package.
32	The portal shall integrate with ORG's grant/loan management software application package.
33	The portal shall support web self-services.
34	The portal shall support XML.
35	The portal support secures data import and export services.
36	The portal shall support digital certificates from authorized issuing agencies.
37	The portal shall integrate with Microsoft Exchange Outlook.
38	The portal shall have the capability to access grant information.
39	The portal shall have the capability to link to the financial data on the grant/loan information.
40	The portal shall support the ability to display financial information created in ORG's reporting writing tool.
41	The portal shall have the capability to drill down to specific line items in ORG's financial system.

Req. #	Search
42	The portal shall allow users to search for all files in the central repository accessible by their rights.
43	The portal shall have the capability to allow users to select and enter search criteria.
44	The portal shall allow the ability to specify keywords within each document based on user specifications.
45	The portal shall have the capability to allow users to search for all files across departments in a central repository, accessible by their rights.
46	The search results shall be displayed in a list by order of search criteria relevance.
47	The portal shall have the capability to search for archived files based on user-specified criteria.
48	The portal shall have the capability to perform a full-text search capability. *Note: Full-text search performs searches within a document.*

Req. #	Content Management System Communication Features (Bulletin Board, Calendars, Discussion Forums)
49	The portal shall have the capability to host a bulletin board accessible to authorized users.
50	The portal shall allow authorized users to post a message on the bulletin board.
51	The portal shall allow authorized users to delete a message on the bulletin board.

Req. #	Content Management System Communication Features (Bulletin Board, Calendars, Discussion Forums)
52	The portal shall have the capability to host an ORG calendar.
53	The portal shall allow authorized users to access organization-wide calendars.
54	The portal shall allow authorized users to add an entry to the organization-wide calendars.
55	The portal shall allow authorized users to update an entry to the organization-wide calendars.
56	The portal shall allow authorized users to delete an entry from organization-wide calendars.
57	The portal shall have the capability to host a department calendar.
58	The portal shall allow authorized users to access department calendars.
59	The portal shall allow authorized users to add an entry to the department calendars.
60	The portal shall allow authorized users to update an entry to the department calendars.
61	The portal shall allow authorized users to delete an entry from department calendars.
62	The portal shall have the capability to access personal Microsoft Outlook calendars.
63	The portal shall allow users to add an entry to their personal calendars.
64	The portal shall allow users to update an entry to their personal calendars.
65	The portal shall allow users to delete an entry to their personal calendars.
66	The portal shall have the capability to host discussion forums.
67	The portal shall allow authorized users to view the discussion forum.
68	The portal shall allow authorized users to post a message in the discussion forum.
69	The portal shall have the capability to allow the organization to contact outside associates.

Req. #	User Profile
70	The portal shall allow a system administrator to set up user profiles.
71	The portal shall allow a system administrator to assign specific access rights to each user profile.
72	The portal shall allow user profiles to be searchable.
73	The portal shall allow authorized users to edit and modify their user profiles.

Req. #	Security
74	The portal shall employ user authentication techniques to restrict access to the portal to authorized users.
75	The portal shall be able to authenticate users at a single point sign-on within the organization.
76	The portal shall provide the capability to assign each user a unique user ID and a temporary password for access.
77	The portal shall require users to change their temporary password after initial login.
78	The portal shall enable the system administrator to reset a password for a user.

(continued)

Table 5.1. *(continued)*

Req. =	Security
79	The portal shall prevent a user from reusing a password for a specified period of time.
80	The portal shall provide the capability for the system administrator to block a user ID after three invalid logon attempts.
81	The portal shall have the capability to protect business-sensitive data.

Req. =	Content Type Requirements Accessible by the Portal
82	Annual reports, past and present
83	Archived e-newsletters
84	Blank evaluation forms
85	Business case documents
86	Business cases
87	Bylaws
88	Loan documents
89	Client activities
90	Communication between ORG and the associates (consultants)
91	Concept papers
92	Confidential associate/consultant evaluations
93	Contract in-progress section
94	Contract signed and approved information
95	HQ financial and operational data and documents
96	Current budget
97	Development plans
98	Strategic plans
99	Employee activity log and schedule
100	Evaluations on programs
101	Expense forms
102	Final contract section
103	Final grantee/loan recipient contract
104	Final versions of proposals and contracts
105	Financial data on the grants/loans
106	Financial information
107	Grant award letters
108	Grant reports
109	IRS determination letter
110	IRS documents
111	Key indicators
112	Key proposals
113	Knowledge forum for consultants to share testimonials and case studies
114	Last year's financials
115	Leases
116	ORG Operating System (FOS) manual
117	List of all projects
118	List of expense codes
119	List of staff
120	List of staff bios

Req. #	Content Type Requirements Accessible by the Portal
121	Industry best practices
122	Legal documents
123	Specific ORG policies and procedures
124	List of staff responsibilities/job descriptions
125	Payroll forms
126	Expense report policies and procedures
127	Phone documents
128	PowerPoint presentations and related handouts
129	Press releases
130	Best training practices
131	Training documents
132	Department-specific procedures
133	Procedures for how expense codes work
134	Project plans
135	Projected versus available funds information
136	Question and answer list
137	Renewal notices
138	Sales information (if any)
139	Searchable index of Q&A topics
140	Data warehousing of social and financial performance data
141	Statistical information about the programs
142	Product knowledge
143	Legal regulations
144	Testimonials
145	Time sheet instructions
146	Trending information
147	Templates
148	Vacation request forms
149	Vouchers

EXPERTISE MANAGEMENT SYSTEMS

A number of organizations prefer to establish expertise locator systems, or "yellow pages" of expertise, in order to locate people with key knowledge and skills for answering questions, forming project teams, collaborating with those of similar interests, and the like. In the private sector, expertise directories within organizations are fairly common. In the public sector, however, it cannot be mandatory, due to existing laws, that a civil servant complete an expertise profile and update it within an expertise directory. Government workers can be encouraged to do it, but it is only voluntary, not mandatory.

A number of software products are available to help construct an expertise directory. Products like AskMe (AskMe Corporation) and ActiveNet (Tacit Corporation) are examples of expertise directory development products. Expert

Seeker is an expertise locator system, developed by Florida International University, in use at NASA's Kennedy Space Center. Most expertise locator systems include profiles of individuals in the organization, and perhaps from outside as well, organized in an easily searchable manner.

ONLINE COMMUNITIES

Another popular knowledge management technique is the use of online communities of practice. Online communities are similar to "birds-of-a-feather" tables, whereby people with interests in a given area can flock together to discuss ideas and share information and knowledge. Online communities typically allow for threaded discussions, posting of documents, polling, and other collaborative features. Online communities are probably the most frequently used application of KM in many organizations. The Federal Aviation Administration, NASA, Best Buy, Hallmark, Computer Sciences Corporation, and many other organizations are actively using online communities. At NASA, the Process Based Mission Assurance Knowledge Management System (PBMA-KMS, pbma.hq.nasa.gov) has a section for work groups, which are online communities. More than ninety active online communities exist on the PBMA-KMS website.

LESSONS-LEARNED SYSTEMS

Many organizations believe in codifying the lessons learned from projects so that they can be shared more easily and in a more structured way than just through word of mouth. Lessons-learned (or best-practice) systems are quite common. The U.S. Department of Energy uses web-based lessons-learned systems and also has a Society for Effective Lessons Learned Sharing (SELLS). The military, through their after-action reviews, have created lessons-learned repositories and centers, such as the Center for Army Lessons Learned (CALL). NASA, through its Lessons Learned Information System (LLIS, llis.nasa.gov), has a lessons-learned repository (as well as a public version, known as PLLS, at llis.nasa.gov) with over one thousand six hundred lessons learned in project management, systems engineering, safety, and many other areas. It's important for these lessons-learned systems to be proactive in lesson analysis and dissemination. Many of these systems fail due to a "pull" approach, or a passive approach to analyzing and disseminating lessons to those who could benefit from their use. Future lessons-learned systems will use intelligent agent technology to "push" appropriate lessons to users where and when they need them.

KNOWLEDGE-SHARING FORUMS

Organizations have accentuated the personalization approaches by using a variety of knowledge-sharing techniques. One approach is to have a knowledge fair or knowledge exchange. Johnson & Johnson and the World Bank have used this approach effectively. Essentially, these sessions are similar to poster sessions in which people gather to discuss their work with other interested colleagues. A variant of this approach is a knowledge-sharing forum in which experienced project managers meet with up-and-coming project leaders to discuss, through storytelling, lessons learned from failures and successes. NASA, through its Academy of Program and Project Leadership (appl.nasa.gov), uses this approach throughout its ten NASA centers. Storytelling or, more formally, "organizational narrative," has become a popular means of sharing knowledge in organizations. Job shadowing, job rotations, and formal mentoring programs are also useful ways of sharing knowledge in organizations.

WHAT TO DO FIRST?

As previously stated, the outcome of the knowledge audit and the needs and goals of the organization will dictate which KM method to use first. For example, if the organization perceives collaboration to be the key problem, then the use of online communities, cross-functional teams, knowledge fairs, and cross-department meetings may be warranted. If knowledge retention is the major issue, then the use of content or document management systems, lessons-learned systems, mentoring programs, and one-on-one knowledge-sharing forums might be the most appropriate KM techniques to apply. If innovation and knowledge creation (i.e., creating new products or services) is the central issue, then a combination of the collaboration and knowledge-sharing approaches above should be considered. As discussed in Wallace Immen's article "Get Creative" (2005), thinking too hard may hinder creativity. Thus, having the time to reflect, letting your mind wander, and relaxing may help bring about creative, innovative ideas.

REFERENCES

Immen, W. (2005), "Get Creative," *The Globe and Mail* (Canada), August 12.
McKeen, J., M. Zack, and S. Singh (2005), "Knowledge Management and Organizational Performance: An Exploratory Survey," Research Paper, The Monieson Centre, School of Business, Queen's University, Canada, June.

Chapter Six

Lessons Learned about Knowledge Management

Knowledge management is for most, but not for everyone. As discussed in the last chapter, some organizations may not be ready to embark on their KM journey due to financial, cultural, and leadership considerations. Other organizations, though, have the vision to see the value of KM and how the organization can innovate through KM.

In the spirit of sharing knowledge, various key lessons can be learned about KM development, strategy, implementation, and management.

KM DEVELOPMENT

Start Small

One of the first lessons in KM development is to start small. You need to control your desire to have a grandiose KM effort, and start with a modest goal, or "low-hanging fruit." Part of the reason for scaling back your effort is to minimize any possible risk of failure and to convince others what KM can offer. Once you build support, it will be easier to expand your KM initiatives. Also, if you pick the "low-hanging fruit" (i.e., the greatest short-term need in the organization where KM can best be applied), the KM project should be successful.

Have a Taxonomy

Whether you build your own taxonomy or you customize one created with software that automatically generates a taxonomy, some standardized set of terms and relationships is needed for KM development and usage. Having a taxonomy will make searches easier and will facilitate maintenance. As the KM system grows, it won't become unwieldy, because a structured taxonomy will enable "smart growth."

Embed KM into Daily Work Life

As a corollary to the previous lesson, KM must be embedded into daily work activities to be successful. Otherwise, if it's something else to do on top of an already full plate, then KM won't be used. Some organizations integrate their KM systems seamlessly through access to their intranet. In this way, they can readily create company-wide online communities, gain access to their expertise locator and knowledge management systems, and provide lessons learned in their best-practice and knowledge repositories. Also, designing for "push" types of features in the KM systems, rather than "pull" approaches, will also encourage usage through active, rather than passive, knowledge dissemination.

Test Pilot before Full Flight

As with any type of project, it is best to do a pilot and get user evaluations and feedback before performing full implementation and deployment. Field-testing the KM system will save headaches down the road. Also, spending the additional time up front in analyzing requirements will save much frustration later in the KM system development cycle. Incorporating proper human-factors design into the KM system will also encourage usability.

Change Management

Change management goes hand in hand with knowledge management. Certain change agents and change management processes will have to be part of the KM strategy and implementation plan. Institutionalizing KM in the organization is very much a cultural process. Transforming individualized learning into organizational learning is a key process that involves change management. Incorporating the people and processes to facilitate this change will be essential in order for KM to succeed in the organization.

Match the KM Technique with the Organizational Culture

The choice of a dominant KM approach for the organization—codification or personalization—depends on the organizational culture. If most employees are fairly introverted and are systems oriented, then they may feel more comfortable with a codification approach. However, if employees are more people oriented, the personalization approach to KM may be best, especially as the first KM technique to solicit endorsement.

For example, one advertising company (Advertising.com) has a very open environment (physically and culturally), with even a "Bring Your Own Dog" philosophy (yes, you can bring your pet to work with you). With their creative, somewhat laid-back approach, an interactive personalization strategy for KM would probably be more amenable to their organizational culture than a structured codification approach.

KM IMPLEMENTATION

Besides KM development, many KM efforts could fail due to poor implementation practices. The following sections will address some lessons learned relating to KM implementation.

Defined KM Roles and Responsibilities

Having defined roles and responsibilities for institutionalizing KM in the organization is crucial. Selecting knowledge stewards to help coordinate KM activities and perhaps appointing knowledge retention managers on major projects could be part of the organizational infrastructure for implementing KM. A chief knowledge officer, or the equivalent, who is placed high on the organizational chart is needed to spearhead the KM initiative in the organization.

Learning from Others

Similar to the theme of the "lessons learned" chapter, KM developers should learn from others who have implemented analogous KM systems within their own or other organizations. Sharing knowledge and learning from others are basic tenets of KM. If a KM implementation fails, an after-action review should be conducted so that others in the organization won't repeat the same mistakes. Posting these lessons in a lessons-learned repository will also help other KM developers in the organization to achieve KM success (check NASA's Lessons Learned Information System at llis.nasa.gov).

Provide Proper User Training and Documentation

As with any type of system, user training is essential in order to ensure familiarity with the new system and ease of use. The use of online tutorials, help desks, one-on-one technical assistance, user training sessions, and the like are important elements of the KM implementation process. The "build it and they will come" philosophy isn't usually the case, as users need to be part of the development and implementation process. Throwing the system over the wall and hoping people will catch it is not a workable solution.

Post-implementation Audit

A good practice to implement is to perform a post-implementation audit about six to twelve months after the KM system has been introduced to see if the system has met its intended goals and objectives. Metrics should have been developed at the beginning of the KM project in order to measure eventual use of the KM system. As part of the post-implementation audit, these metrics should be calculated to see, for example, if worker productivity has improved, if employees' searching for "lost" information and knowledge has lessened, or if knowledge retention and sharing have improved.

KM STRATEGY

Aside from lessons learned from KM development and implementation, another important area where best practices can be gleaned is KM strategy. Here are a few key lessons learned on this topic.

Be Aligned

Many KM efforts may fail due to not aligning the KM plan with the business's strategic mission and goals. It is similar to the issue of verification and validation. Are the KM developers building the "right" system, and are they building the system "right"? Relating to KM strategy, the design of a KM plan may look wonderful, but if it doesn't fit the organizational goals and objectives, then it will probably fail due to not tying the outcomes to the business's strategic goals. If there is a disconnect, then KM will operate in isolation and won't permeate the organization. KM must cut across the functional silos of the organization and be integrated within the organization's strategic goals.

Figure 6.1 shows an example of aligning the KM strategy and plan with the organizational strategy. Moving from left to right in figure 6.1, the organization's strategic goals are indicated, and the KM strategy, goals, and implementation components are then linked to the organizational strategy.

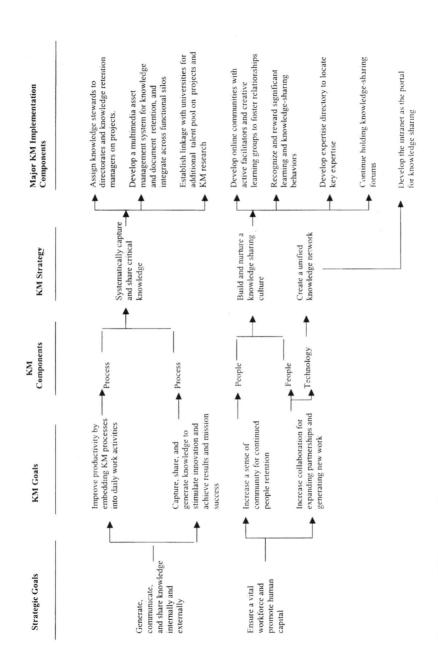

Strategic Goals

Generate, communicate, and share knowledge internally and externally

Ensure a vital workforce and promote human capital

KM Goals

Improve productivity by embedding KM processes into daily work activities

Capture, share, and generate knowledge to stimulate innovation and achieve results and mission success

Increase a sense of community for continued people retention

Increase collaboration for expanding partnerships and generating new work

KM Components

Process

Process

People

People

Technology

KM Strategy

Systematically capture and share critical knowledge

Build and nurture a knowledge sharing culture

Create a unified knowledge network

Major KM Implementation Components

Assign knowledge stewards to directorates and knowledge retention managers on projects.

Develop a multimedia asset management system for knowledge and document retention, and integrate across functional silos

Establish linkage with universities for additional talent pool on projects and KM research

Develop online communities with active facilitators and creative learning groups to foster relationships

Recognize and reward significant learning and knowledge-sharing behaviors

Develop expertise directory to locate key expertise

Continue holding knowledge-sharing forums

Develop the intranet as the portal for knowledge sharing

Figure 6.1. KM Strategy Alignment.

Recognize and Reward

A recognition and reward system should be an integral component of the KM strategy. Extrinsic motivation may play a role, but the desire is to create intrinsic motivation through KM. People like to be recognized (and rewarded), and ways to promote recognition are important to achieving organizational and KM success. Some organizations use awards, gifts, newsletters including updates on whose "lesson" was most frequently accessed during a given month, and other techniques to encourage use of the KM system. Some organizations, such as the World Bank, have even developed learning and knowledge-sharing proficiencies as part of the annual job performance appraisal. In this way, people are measured for how well they learn and share knowledge with others.

Technology and Organizational Strategy for KM

As mentioned previously, KM is about 80 percent people, process, and culture, and the other 20 percent is technology. Technology enables people to share knowledge, through web-based and intranet technologies. Both the technology strategy and the organizational strategy for KM need to be developed in concert in order for KM to have a long, useful life.

Use Bottom-Up and Top-Down Approaches

KM needs both top-down and bottom-up approaches to be successful in an organization. Top-down refers to starting the KM initiative with senior leadership and pushing it down through the organization. Senior management champions are critical to the success of the KM effort. Bottom-up refers to situations in which potential KM users see the value in KM and tell their managers, who in turn enlighten senior leadership as to the value of KM. This bidirectional enthusiasm enables an organization to realize the full potential of KM.

KM MANAGEMENT

Key lessons from KM strategy, development, and implementation have been presented in previous chapters, and some insights from managing a KM project should also be discussed. Here are some important lessons on KM management.

Use Good Project Management

As with any type of project, whether knowledge management based or not, good project management principles and practices should be applied. Budgets, schedules, resource plans, and measurement tools should be developed for the KM project. Project reviews should be used during the KM project development cycle. A project team leader should be appointed, and weekly project status reports should be issued.

Spread the Word

Educating employees about knowledge management should be a part of the KM management team's strategy. Some skepticism of KM will exist, and others will just be ignorant of what KM is all about. As the KM initiative unfolds, the KM project team needs to keep people involved by eliciting user feedback during introduction of iterative versions of the KM system, and the team also needs to give KM tutorials to further educate the organization about KM. Once the KM system has achieved some results, the KM project team should market these results throughout the organization to further create interest in KM and show how KM helps achieve organizational goals.

Cross-Functional Teaming

In order to secure the best representation across the organization for the KM initiative, cross-functional teaming could be a helpful management strategy. This would allow representatives from the various departments and divisions to be part of the KM effort. This enables cross-fertilization of ideas within the organization and attempts to knock down functional silos. Also, getting well-respected department or division representatives on the team will add credibility to the KM effort and will encourage support from others in their respective departments or divisions.

WHAT *NOT* TO DO!

The previous lessons will help information and library science professionals get on the right track with their KM projects. Here are some other suggestions that should be followed with respect to KM:

- Don't force-fit user requirements to the KM system.
- Don't call every technology tool a KM tool.
- Don't convince people that KM will answer all your problems.
- Don't overpromise.
- Don't develop KM in isolation of the business strategy.
- Don't say you are a KM expert without proper education and training on KM methodologies, techniques, processes, and tools.
- Don't develop KM approaches without having metrics in mind.

A GOOD KM STRATEGY

A good KM strategy to follow is to embed knowledge management within strategic human capital management in the organization. Linking KM to the strategic management of human capital can provide great synergies. In this manner, KM will serve as a key pillar underpinning a human capital strategy for the organization. Most senior leaders can appreciate the need for retaining and recruiting employees and capturing key knowledge before it leaves the organization. Here, human capital (i.e., people) in the organization seems more tangible than knowledge management. KM may seem amorphous to many individuals, so weaving it into a human capital strategy for the organization may be a wise approach.

In fact, the U.S. federal government is incorporating KM into their human capital strategies for the agencies. Some other key pillars for forming a human capital strategy are competency management, performance management, and change management. Competency management refers to determining and developing the knowledge and skill areas of the organization's workforce for the future. Performance management deals with providing the mechanisms for recognizing and rewarding people for performance, as well as accounting for lack of performance. Change management provides techniques and processes for introducing change in the organization through a performance-oriented and knowledge-sharing culture.

SUMMARY

This chapter provided some "lessons learned" about "lessons learned" in knowledge management. These practical guidelines and insights should help you, as part of your KM team, to ensure success in your KM initiative. The development, implementation, management, and strategy of KM are essential elements as you embark on your KM journey.

Chapter Seven

Showing Value from Knowledge Management

In today's competitive environment, executives want to know the bottom line or the return on investment (ROI) as part of any business case presented to them. With knowledge management, quantifying the intangible assets (i.e., human capital, structural capital, and social capital) may be an arduous task. In fact, some organizations are using the term "return on vision" instead of "return on investment" for their knowledge management projects.

As discussed in an earlier chapter, organizations typically present a business case to get management to "buy into" a project, whether there is a formal or an informal KM program in the organization. Part of this business case should include metrics for measuring the expected value to be added by the KM project. The "show me the money" statement is often voiced by senior management in terms of their possible endorsement of a KM project.

This chapter will take a look at some of the possible metrics and measures to use in order to show value from knowledge management.

THE FINANCE AND ACCOUNTING PERSPECTIVE

Baruch Lev of New York University, Nick Bontis of McMaster University in Canada, and others have used finance and accounting approaches to quantify intangible assets and intellectual capital. In interviews, as highlighted in Juergen Daum's book *Intangible Assets and Value Creation* (2003), Baruch Lev points out that one of the major problems with today's accounting systems is that they are still based on transactions rather than on the value-creation or innovation process (Daum 2002). Lev discusses the need for a new accounting system, a Value Chain Blueprint, that relates more to a knowledge economy. He points out the need for managers to be able to assess the expected return on R&D investment, employee training, brand enhancement, and other intangibles and compare these returns with those of physical investment.

Leif Edvinsson, formerly the director of intellectual capital at Skandia in Sweden, believes that organizations need to pay more attention to structural capital—the intangibles left behind when people go home from the office (Daum 2001). Skandia developed the Navigator report to accompany their annual stockholder report. The Navigator uses a balanced scorecard approach (see Robert Kaplan and David Norton's book *Strategy Maps* [2004]) to measure customer relations, internal processes, human capital, and financial results. In this manner, a more true representation of a company's value can be determined.

Others have used an activity-based costing (ABC) approach to value intangible assets. According to Value Based Management.net (www.value-basedmanagement.net), this technique assigns cost drivers based on the number of events or transactions involved in the process of providing a product or service. In his book *Valuating Information Intangibles: Measuring the Bottom Line Contributions of Librarians and Information Professionals* (2000), Frank Portugal discusses the knowledge-value-added idea, which applies a surrogate measure for determining how much of any intangible asset—knowledge—is embedded in each subprocess that leads to a specific product or service.

THE HUMAN RESOURCE ACCOUNTING PERSPECTIVE

Besides the financial and accounting views on measuring intangible assets as related to knowledge management, the human resources (HR) community has applied some HR accounting techniques to quantifying intangible assets. One of the leading individuals in this community is Eric Flamholtz of UCLA. As Flamholtz describes in his article "Measuring the ROI of Management Development" (2003), the human and intellectual capital in an organization are the core economic resources. Flamholtz advocates the use of a stochastic rewards valuation model for measuring the value of investments in training programs. He discusses a five-step approach for this model:

1. Define the mutually exclusive set of states, or service states, an individual may occupy in the organizational system, or organization.
2. Determine the value of each state to the organization, or the service state values.
3. Estimate a person's expected tenure, or service life, in the organization.

4. Find the probability that a person will occupy each possible state at specified future times.
5. Discount the expected future cash flows to determine their present value.

Nick Bontis emphasizes the need for quantitative and qualitative measures for human capital (see "Accounting for Knowledge," *CMA Management*, www.managementmag.com). For example, turnover figures, exit interviews, training and development investment, audits looking at e-mail traffic to identify organizational information flows, structural equation models, causal models, and other techniques and measures can be very helpful for determining the value of knowledge management.

THE IT PERSPECTIVE

As knowledge management has grown partly out of the information technology (IT) field, information technologists also have applied their background in developing metrics for knowledge management. Susan Hanley, formerly of Dell, developed some KM performance measures for the U.S. Navy, based on an IT systems perspective, as shown in table 7.1 (http://km.gov).

I have also developed some KM metrics based on fuzzy logic. Fuzzy logic is part of the field of soft computing, in which "possibility" theory and "uncrisp reasoning" are used instead of probability theory and "crisp" reasoning. Since many of the KM benefits are soft measures, fuzzy logic may be ideally suited for converting these soft measures into hard ones. I discuss this approach in my paper "Developing Metrics for Determining KM Success: A Fuzzy Logic Approach" (2005). For example, a KM effort can improve employee morale. If we define employee morale as the perceived degree of employee interaction in the organization, fuzzy logic concepts can be applied to develop a fuzzy set for employee morale as follows:

- No interaction occurs ("F"): 0.00
- People ask other employees to join them for lunch ("E"): 0.20
- Employees share knowledge within departments ("D"): 0.40
- Employees share knowledge with others across departments ("C"): 0.60
- Communities of practice are flourishing ("B"): 0.80
- All employees are connected with everyone else in the organization ("A"): 1.00

Table 7.1. Summary of KM Performance Measures in Personnel and Training (U.S. Navy, 2001: *Knowledge Management Metrics Guide*, Washington, D.C., www.km.gov)

KM Initiatives	Systems Measures	Output Measures	Outcome Measures
Portal • For HR functions	**Common Measures** • Searching precision and recall • Usage of personalization features • Frequency of general search versus use of predefined links • Number of users with the portal as their "home page"	**Common Measures** • Printed communications cost (reduced costs for printed newsletters) • Time spent "gathering" information	• Reduced time to find relevant information • Reduced training time or learning curve (if portal is used to integrate multiple separate systems)
Communities of Practice • Ex-patriots • People who are involved in a change of duty station • Functional by expertise	**Common Measures** • Number of contributions • Frequency of update • Ratio of the number of members to the number of contributors (conversion rate) • Number of members	**Common Measures** • Number of grievances • Attrition or turnover rate • Ratio or number of offers extended to number of offers accepted for employment	• Decreased attrition or turnover rate • Increase in number of offers to number of accepted offers of employment • Increased employee satisfaction • Savings and/or improvement in organizational quality and efficiency
E-learning	**Common Measures** • Number of courses taken/use	**Common Measures** • Training costs	• Savings and/or improvement in organizational quality and efficiency • Improved employee satisfaction • Reduced cost of training

THE ORGANIZATIONAL DEVELOPMENT PERSPECTIVE

Aside from the IT, finance, accounting, and HR approaches to measuring intangible assets, the organizational development (OD) community has applied some organizational learning metrics to knowledge management. For example, competency models, subsystem performance, and business process auditing may be techniques applied to value intangible assets. The Montague Institute (1997) describes these techniques as:

Competency models: By classifying the behaviors of "successful" employees and calculating the market value of their output, a dollar value can be assigned to the intellectual capital they create and use in their work.

Subsystem performance: Quantify success or progress in one intellectual capital component.

Business process auditing: Measure how information enhances value in a given business process.

Verna Allee, in her paper "A Value Network Approach for Modeling and Measuring Intangibles" (2002), states that intangibles are at the heart of all human activity, especially socioeconomic activity. Allee views organizations as value networks, whereby a web of relationships generates tangible and intangible value through complex dynamic exchanges between two or more individuals, groups, or organizations. Allee uses mapping techniques to visualize these connections and then uses value creation analysis to determine the cost and benefit of each value-creating activity.

KM METRICS: SOME EXAMPLES

As we discussed in an earlier chapter, there are a number of key factors that explain why organizations embark on KM initiatives. They can be grouped into five general categories: adaptability/agility, creativity, institutional memory building, organizational *internal* effectiveness, and organizational *external* effectiveness. Let's look at how we can quantify some of the key factors under each category.

For adaptability and agility, some of the key factors that contribute to this area are the ability to adapt quickly to unanticipated changes and the ability to anticipate potential market opportunities for new products and services. One way to measure the ability to adapt quickly to anticipated changes is to look at market response times. This could be determined by the duration of time from when a market condition was triggered until the organization adjusted to this new market condition based upon some desired level of performance. As new changes are implemented to react to market trends, the organization's market response times can be measured and hopefully will decrease to show the agility of the organization. In a related manner, organizations need early-warning systems in place to anticipate possible surprises affecting the organization. Trying to account, in advance, for signs of risk and the exposure that an organization faces to such risks is where early-warning systems can help. Changing the executives' mindsets is crucial for handling unexpected surprises.

For creativity, some organizations may look at their speed of innovation of new products or services or their ability to identify new business opportunities. Buckman Labs used a target number of 80 percent as the fraction of their employees who should be involved with the customer in some meaningful way. By having more employees with a direct, close relationship with the customer, the possibility of new ideas generated from customer interaction should increase. Customer relationships should also improve, and the development of new products or services can then be tracked. "Learning the hard way" can also be tracked by measuring costs and schedule overruns related to not learning from others or by using lessons-learned systems. Dennis Lee, a spacecraft systems engineer at NASA's Goddard Space Flight Center, describes a situation in which NASA's Lessons Learned Information System (LLIS) wasn't consulted and costs and schedule overruns resulted due to not accessing the LLIS:

> The risks are a technical problem that has yet to happen, and in that context of risk identification, project managers and technical managers need to have some insight and visibility into these risks, and that's where the lessons learned information system comes into play. One specific example that I wanted to relate here was the HESSI Sine vibrations problem that occurred in January of 2000. At that time, the HESSI SMEX (Small Explorer) project was moving to the random sine vibration NASA test facility on its way to a July 2000 launch. As a result of an equipment problem at the test facility, the flight hardware was severely damaged, which caused the project to come to a halt. As a result of that, I reviewed the Lessons Learned Information System, and did a search using the existing Lessons Learned Information System to search on key words, as it's set up to do, "vibration testing." And I found a citation in there that was directly applicable to the HESSI vibration test failure. And that clued me into the value of the Lessons Learned Information System. This particular citation was directed at the test facility where HESSI was planning to do their testing, and did their testing, as well as identified the very test equipment that was used by HESSI, and where HESSI's mishap investigation board focused on. It alerted me to the value of Lessons Learned Information System. And I realized that risk management is a process that needs to be done continuously throughout a spacecraft project life cycle. And using the Lessons Learned Information System will support the engineers and the project managers in assessing and mitigating their risks. (pbma.hq.nasa .gov/videolibrary/index.php?fuseaction=videolibrary.transcript&vid=293)

Another category for creating value through knowledge management is institutional memory building. Knowledge retention and recruiting talented employees can contribute to building the organization's institutional memory. Capturing of best practices can be tracked by seeing if the number of best practices codified in the organization's repository increases over time. Also, testimonials from individuals who are the recipients of such lessons can be obtained in order to assess the value added by these lessons. Of course, recruiting and retaining talented employees can be tracked as well—for example, the number of employees with advanced degrees could influence the talent pool and innovation in the organization.

In terms of organizational internal effectiveness, some factors can be easily traced, such as reduced redundancy of information and knowledge, improvements in profits and increased revenue, shorter product development cycles, and expanded training and development opportunities. Even an increased sense of belonging among the employees and an improved communications flow can be assessed through culture surveys and focus groups.

For organizational external effectiveness, increasing customer satisfaction and better managing of customer relationships can be measured through customer feedback surveys, telephone calls, focus groups, and sales numbers. Improvement of strategic alliances can also be partly determined by the number of mergers and acquisitions the organization makes.

MACRO-KM MEASUREMENT

Up to now, we have been discussing micro-KM measurement, that is, measurement of KM initiatives in the firm or organization. A number of researchers, such as Nick Bontis of McMaster University and Yogesh Malhotra of Syracuse University, have gone beyond the organization level and have developed intellectual capital models that examine national or countrywide innovation performance. One reason for looking at macro-KM measurement is to better see the effects of KM beyond just the internal influences on organizations. For example, Bontis (2003) has looked at Canada's innovation performance by using the following indicators:

- Knowledge Performance (R&D investment, business investment in R&D, and innovation output)
- Skills Development (education, access)
- Innovation Environment (tax, venture capital)
- Community Innovation (localized clusters)

Bontis later extended his work to develop a National Intellectual Capital Index. In his article "National Intellectual Capital Index: A United Nations Initiative for the Arab Region" (2004), Bontis indicates that this index consists of four components: human capital, process capital, renewal capital, and market capital. Bontis's findings from his research are that human capital is the key antecedent for the intellectual wealth of a nation and that a strong link exists between national intellectual capital and financial capital.

Yogesh Malhotra, in his work at the United Nations (2003), has also worked on national knowledge systems and has developed a Balanced Scorecard approach for knowledge assets measurement and management (http://unpan1 .un.org/intradoc/groups/public/documents/un/unpan011601.pdf). Malhotra looks at the following factors:

Knowledge Management (Learning and Growth): Competencies to change, improve, and innovate

Process Improvement (Business Processes): Competencies to transform business processes

Budget and Cost Management (Value Creation): Competencies to create value—socioeconomic and developmental

Relationship Management (Stakeholders): Competencies to create stakeholder loyalty through value-added services

Vision and Strategy: Defining the national vision of the knowledge-based economy

THE TRANSFORMED LIBRARY SPECIALIST: THE KNOWLEDGE MANAGER

Today's library specialist will continue to take on more knowledge management roles and skills. In a posting in the Special Libraries Association Career Center on August 11, 2005 (sla.jobcontrolcenter.com), the responsibilities for a Knowledge Manager at Amylin Pharmaceutical in San Diego are shown as:

> Responsible for leading a company knowledge management initiative aimed toward bringing information and knowledge together to ensure that it is easily accessible to users. Defines how information is organized and accessed within Amylin's data and knowledge repositories. Leads the development and implementation of solutions and projects related to Knowledge, Content, and Document management. Have ability to recommend functional or technical solutions to Knowledge Management issues. Communicates and negotiates with vendors for the selection and purchase of knowledge and content management solutions. Oversees the content strategies, usability, and design of the company intranet and electronic document management system (Livelink). Assists

with the review and edit of corporate intranet site content to ensure content is appropriate and up to date. Develops, implements, and maintains a global information architecture (taxonomy) for documents and data. Selects, implements, and maintains enterprise search and retrieval solutions. Conducts information gathering interviews and audits to define where knowledge repositories are located. Gathers and organizes information from appropriate sources and individuals into easily retrievable formats. Provides instruction and support to employees on use of knowledge and content tools and technologies. Stays abreast of current trends and technologies in the information, knowledge, and content management fields. Assists with the evaluation and selection of external information resources. Conducts online searches. Assists with other library or information services projects and tasks as required. May supervise staff.

The requirements are:

Required: an advanced degree in library or information science or equivalent experience and education with 8+ years of related work experience. Have knowledge of current and emerging information technologies for the retrieval, development, and dissemination of information. Must have experience deploying information/knowledge management solutions in a corporate environment. Have knowledge of web user interfaces related to information management retrieval systems. Proven experience with defining classification systems for documents as well as data. Experience with enterprise content and document management systems such as SharePoint and Livelink. Have understanding of Knowledge, Content, and Information Management theory, practice, and program development. Experience with search and retrieval using a variety of online systems (Dialog, STN, Ovid). Knowledge of Internet and print resources in the biotechnology and pharmaceutical industry desired. Experience with information management technologies, such as data warehouse, executive information system, data mining, business intelligence, and enterprise portals a plus. Excellent communication, organizational, and project management skills.

From the above job description for a knowledge manager, we can see that the types of skills and knowledge that a library or information professional possesses are quite applicable to the role of knowledge manager. The ability to organize information and knowledge is a typical task that a library specialist can perform. Extending these functions into selecting and developing knowledge, content, or document management systems is something that more library and information professionals will be asked to do in the near future. One area that is not included in the knowledge manager position description above but is increasingly important is the need to evaluate the KM system and associated KM initiatives. This is where knowledge of KM metrics, as described throughout this chapter, will come into play.

SUMMARY

As discussed in this chapter and others, the library and information professional's role is being transformed. Knowledge management will be increasingly important and will broaden the scope of the library specialist's responsibilities. Library and information professionals need to have a proactive involvement in the knowledge management field, as their backgrounds can help further shape the knowledge management area. The use of metrics for showing the value of knowledge management initiatives will continue to be a primary component in determining the success of KM in organizations.

REFERENCES

Allee, V. (2002). "A Value Network Approach for Modeling and Measuring Intangibles," paper presented at the Transparent Enterprise Conference, Madrid, November.

Bontis, N. (2003). "Canada's Innovation Performance: A Preliminary Benchmarking within the OECD," White Paper, McMaster University, www.bontis.com, May 27.

Bontis, N. (2004). "National Intellectual Capital Index: A United Nations Initiative for the Arab Region," *Journal of Intellectual Capital*, Vol. 5, No. 1, Emerald Publishing.

Daum, J. (2001), *New Economy Analyst Report*, www.juergendaum.com, November 13.

Daum, J. (2002), *New Economy Analyst Report*, www.juergendaum.com, March 6.

Daum, J. (2003), *Intangible Assets and Value Creation*, John Wiley, New York.

Flamholtz, E. (2003), "Putting Balance and Validity into the Balanced Scorecard," *Journal of Human Resource Costing and Accounting*, Vol. 7, No. 3, Autumn.

Kaplan, R., and D. Norton (2004), *Strategy Maps*, Harvard Business School Press, Cambridge, Mass.

Liebowitz, J. (2005), "Developing Metrics for Determining KM Success: A Fuzzy Logic Approach," *Issues of Information Systems: IACIS-05 Proceedings*, International Association for Computer Information Systems, www.iacis.org, October.

Malhotra, Y. (2003), "Expanding Public Space for the Development of the Knowledge Society," Report by the Ad Hoc Expert Group Meeting on Knowledge Systems for Development, United Nations Development Program, New York, September 4–5, unpan1.un.org/intradoc/groups/public/documents/un/unpan014138.pdf.

Montague Institute (1997), "Measuring Intellectual Assets," www.montague.com, March.

Portugal, F. (2000), *Valuating Information Intangibles: Measuring the Bottom Line Contributions of Librarians and Information Professionals*, Special Libraries Association, Washington, D.C.

Chapter Eight

The Future of
Knowledge Management

What's Next?

Knowledge management has lasting value due to its inherently good qualities, but it will probably never become a separate discipline. It will be woven into such fields as organizational learning, computer science, management, and systems analysis. Knowledge management is a multidisciplinary field and, as such, borrows and adapts techniques and processes from many areas, such as those mentioned above. In the same way that business process improvement, customer relationship management, and supply chain management are being woven into the fabric of the organization, knowledge management is following the same path.

In many organizations, especially the government, knowledge management is being subsumed within the organization's strategic human capital plan. The U.S. Government Accountability Office (GAO) report on lessons learned from human capital initiatives, in appendix B, provides some interesting insights on the critical success factors for human capital strategy, and how knowledge management can contribute to this strategy. Other organizations are weaving knowledge management into their human resources division and are accentuating the use of knowledge-sharing proficiencies in the organization. Still others are integrating knowledge management within their information technology (IT) division, through the use of intranets and web-based technologies.

Knowledge management will always have altruistic value, as any senior leader knows that retaining and leveraging key expertise is vital for the longevity of an organization. Additionally, improving a sense of community and belonging through knowledge management allows employee morale to increase, which ultimately increases worker productivity, sales, innovation, and other important growth factors. The often intangible nature of knowledge management makes it difficult, at times, to justify expending dollars for a seemingly "soft" benefit versus a "hard" one (such as spending money to buy a new piece of equipment). The previous chapter highlighted the need for developing KM metrics in order to quantify some of these "soft" values.

The other challenge for knowledge management is to apply more rigor to the field so that it becomes more of a science and less of an art. Of course, there will always be elements of both art and science in the knowledge management field. However, KM development methodologies, techniques, processes, and tools must continue to be constructed and applied so that KM isn't using ad hoc types of methods. Social network analysis, knowledge audit instruments, KM development and implementation methodologies, and various KM standards need to be applied in order to give KM more solidity and thus more permanency.

Library and information professionals' roles and responsibilities will continue to transform using knowledge management functions. The "collection" and "connection" of information and knowledge will always be important within an organization, no matter what they are called. Library specialists will continue to have an active role in the "collection" piece of KM and could play a role in the "connection" of people to people and people to resources within the organization. The library specialist will continue to serve as a broker in linking the right people to the right resources at the right time. The library professional will also be involved in taxonomy development and the ongoing development of knowledge, content, and document management systems.

WHERE ARE THE REAL BANGS FOR THE BUCK IN KM?

Pushing knowledge management closer to the front line is where tremendous benefits will be reaped from KM. Leveraging knowledge from the customer and moving new knowledge closer to the customer is where KM can help and organizations can prosper. Hallmark has experienced this phenomenon through online communities, whereby new ideas for greeting cards emanate from customers directly to Hallmark. Increased innovation and improved customer satisfaction will typically result by pushing knowledge closer to the customer and having ways of easily pulling knowledge from the customer to the organization.

Enterprise content management systems (ECMs) are where many organizations have invested in knowledge management. Most organizations have recognized the importance of more easily locating information and knowledge and being able to quickly respond to requests for proposals, questions from customers and employees, and the like. Through ECMs, organizations have improved systems to search, retrieve, and store documents and knowledge bases.

Knowledge capture and knowledge retention activities will continue to be an important part of KM for organizations to embrace. Certainly, knowledge retention activities can be codified and made part of the organization's ECM. However, the personalization approach to KM also needs to be fostered to allow knowledge sharing to take place from a people perspective. Whether using mentoring programs, knowledge-sharing forums, knowledge exchanges/fairs, job rotations, shadowing, or other programs, the personalization approach to capturing and sharing knowledge will also need to exist. Building the institutional memory of the organization, especially trying to capture the rationale behind how decisions were reached, will continue to be a key part of KM in organizations.

Online communities of practice are probably the most used application of KM today. These communities allow sharing of ideas and ways to easily answer questions. They also allow posting of documents, polling of questions, and ways to link people having similar interests. Many of the leading organizations today use online communities, and this trend will continue in the future. Now, there are various websites, like www.thefacebook.com, that use social networks to link college students with those of similar interests at their college or others.

Besides online communities, expertise locators or "yellow pages" of experts will be a typical feature on most organizations' intranet sites. In this manner, employees will be able to locate other employees who have designated expertise in particular areas for forming project teams, to link with others of similar interests, and even to reach out to experts outside the organization. Private industry typically has expertise locators. In the government, developing an expert profile and keeping it up to date and posted on the expertise locator system can be only voluntary, due to privacy laws, instead of mandatory, as in industry. However, other not-for-profits, such as foundations, are actively developing expertise locator systems.

WHAT'S BEYOND KM?

Today's younger generation of workers are used to cell phones, personal digital assistants (PDAs), iPods, computers, DVD players, e-mail, virtual reality, videoconferencing, telecommuting, instant messaging, faxes, chat rooms, online communities, e-learning, wireless routers, and so on. To me, life has become more complex as the number of in-boxes has increased, and with an electronic umbilical cord, people can reach you anytime, anyplace. Also, with access to e-mail, people almost expect that you are on e-mail twenty-four hours, seven days a week, and want an almost instantaneous reply to their message. Whatever happened to the good ole days when life wasn't so fast paced, complicated, and demanding?

Unfortunately, the years ahead don't look much better. Certainly, through KM, we can work smarter, not harder. However, it seems that we are spending additional time in working both smarter and harder. Let's take an example. Even though an individual can be more productive through KM, that individual is probably still spending the same number of hours, or more, at the office in order to get farther ahead on the promotion ladder. It's the simple case of "let's see how much more I can do"—and KM can help achieve that goal.

We even see new transformations happening in K–12 education—so much that we need improved ways of measuring returns on investment for the application of new technologies in the classroom. The topic of return on investment in the use of technology by educational organizations, specifically K–12, is an important area of interest that is gaining the attention of legislators, educators, parents, and the private sector. With the No Child Left Behind Act, the use of digital instruction devices becomes ever more paramount in terms of creating a potential digital divide in the United States. With the creation of national and regional technology standards, schools are hard pressed to prepare their students for the technological skills needed in the workplace. One technique that is starting to be used more in K–12 education is the use of personal digital assistants (PDAs), even in lieu of personal computers. With wireless technologies, PDAs can access e-mail and the Internet, and they are becoming more powerful with each new PDA generation developed. With space limitations in many schools, a number of schools have found it difficult to provide a desktop computer for every student. The PDA alternative is starting to be used more widely as a tool for students, and it offers a creative approach for using the PDA at the site of instruction (the student's desk), rather than having to relocate one's class to a computer lab. PDAs also allow students to easily collect data outside of the classroom, whether on a field trip or simply outdoors. Granted, there are costs associated with using PDAs, but some schools have found that the advantages seem to outweigh the disadvantages.

For example, PDAs are being used in K–12 classrooms in many ways. At the Consolidated High School District 230 in Orland Park, Illinois, high school students are utilizing PDAs and attachable sensors to monitor pH levels, temperature, dissolved oxygen, heat, and other qualities at a nearby pond. Fifth-grade science students in Madison Heights, Michigan, are utilizing PDAs to create nature journals and field guides of their schoolyard and communities. Junior high school students in math classes in Tinley Park, Illinois, are loading math and stock market games onto their PDAs. Language arts students in Kentucky are using e-books on their PDAs and can create their own e-books and post them on the Internet. PDAs are being used as research tools by social studies and journalism students in elementary and middle schools in Louisiana and Washington. And special education students in Marysville, Kansas, and Larchmont, New York, are benefiting from using PDAs for their organizational capabilities (http://www.glencoe.com/sec/teachingtoday/educationupclose.phtml/14).

Some schools are offering payment plans to students (e.g., twenty-five dollars per month) so that students can purchase a PDA. Educational gift programs, like Palm's Education Pioneer Grants, are also available through PDA manufacturers, and corporate sponsors (and the National Science Foundation) are providing money for using handhelds in schools. A key issue that surfaces with PDAs is, are the PDAs worth the money? In other words, what kind of return on investment can be determined for the use of PDAs in the classroom for K–12 instruction?

We have seen the same types of questions being asked in the KM arena — is KM worth the investment? By including KM as one of the key pillars of an organization's human capital strategy, this question can be answered more easily; however, as we have previously discussed, new measures and a return-on-investment methodology must be developed for KM to show value.

According to Jonathan Spira and Joshua Feintuch's article "The Cost of Not Paying Attention: How Interruptions Impact Knowledge Worker Productivity" (2005), unnecessary interruptions account for about 28 percent of the knowledge worker's day, which translates to a cost of about $588 billion per year for U.S. companies. Some of these interruptions are due to not being able to find the right information or the right person to address one's question. This is where knowledge management can help, as it should be easier to locate the right resource at the right time through enterprise content management systems, portals, expertise locators, online communities, and the like. Thomas Davenport of Babson College (Davenport and Beck 2001) talks about the "attention economy" as a follow-on to knowledge management, where the goal is how to get the attention of a senior executive, especially with the deluge of e-mails, memos, telephone calls, PDA messages, and other sources of information. In their book *Attention Economy* (2001), Tom Davenport and John Beck state that understanding and managing attention is the single most important determinant of business success. They talk about "attention-conscious knowledge management" that is highly conscious of the audience's attention. Davenport and Beck indicate that knowledge managers at Accenture, for example, are trying to produce more attention-getting knowledge or are protecting employees' attention by eliminating unnecessary distributions of knowledge and information.

Another growing trend is the merging of knowledge management, business intelligence, and competitive intelligence into what I call strategic intelligence. In my book *Strategic Intelligence: Business Intelligence, Competitive Intelligence, and Knowledge Management* (2006), I describe strategic intelligence as the ability to make effective strategic decisions in an organization through the synergy of knowledge management, business intelligence, and competitive intelligence. Producing and leveraging valuable knowledge internally and externally can help the decision maker to make the right decisions.

THE LIBRARY PROFESSIONAL'S ROLE IN THE FUTURE

As knowledge management continues to permeate the library professional's environment, I envision the following types of scenarios. A typical day in the life of a library professional will include such activities as contributing toward the content and organization of multimedia asset management systems. These web-based, searchable repositories would include webcasts of lectures and symposia given at the organization (whether it is a corporation, university, public library, or other organization); PowerPoint slides of briefings given throughout the organization; proposals; videotapes, CDs, and DVDs that can be searched through speech-to-text translation; company documents and manuals; video nuggets of key organization experts explaining their lessons learned and insights; company tutorials; and other media. The library professional will be involved in the population, organization, and distribution of information and knowledge, as it pertains to these types of knowledge management systems and others. In corporations, the human resources department will likely have the role of maintaining and expanding (along with the IT department) the organization's expertise locator system. In educational institutions, the library is a likely owner of such a system. The library professional will continue to be proactive in sending appropriate information to employees in the organization that can best benefit from it. This is in contrast to being just reactive and responding to requests from employees.

Many knowledge management systems have a news-feed feature whereby the user clicks the areas in which he or she would like to receive daily news that relates to his or her areas of interest. The "my" version of the knowledge management system will be tailored to fit the user's profile. The library professional will be involved in making the arrangements between news sources and the organization so that employees can be kept up to date on a daily basis.

Unfortunately, many library functions are being targeted for outsourcing or competitive sourcing (A-76 in the U.S. government). In the U.S. government, this could eliminate many civil servants who are working in the libraries and replace them with contractors. The library has been changing over the years. At universities, libraries often have coffee bars and gathering places in order to stimulate social interaction and discussion and perhaps lure students to the physical spaces of the library. With digital libraries and many articles that can be easily accessed online, the library has transformed significantly over the years. Thirty years ago, doctoral students had to physically roam through the library stacks and find the articles, periodicals, and books they needed for their dissertation research. Today, with access to electronic resources as part of a university's library subscription, articles can be located and received with the press of a button.

Library professionals of the future will continue to possess the necessary skills in organizing, cataloging, and managing information, but their knowledge base will be enhanced by the need to further integrate information technology and knowledge management functions within their daily work. Library professionals of the future will be more savvy than today's library specialists, as the environment will continue to change and evolve. Library professionals will be asked to take on leadership roles, versus simply support roles, in making knowledge management a reality in many organizations. They will increasingly become more proactive in order to keep pace with the changing times and to allow organizations to become more agile.

The years ahead look promising as knowledge management further infiltrates the library and organizational life. However, caution is advised, as one shouldn't put all one's eggs in one basket. Knowledge management will be woven into the fabric of the organization, and other new initiatives will surface. The library can take a partial ownership role in knowledge management but should continue to explore new ways of thinking, expanding, and building the organizational learning capabilities in order to make the organization more flexible, adaptable, and successful in the future.

Information and library professionals should continue to hone their skills to become KM practitioners. By integrating their technical skills with their organizational talents, library professionals can transform themselves into KM practitioners. Specifically, by being sensitive to the people, process, culture, and technology components of KM, library professionals can be key players on the KM team. They will then be able to influence their organization and transform the adage "knowledge is power" to "*sharing* knowledge is power."

REFERENCES

Davenport, T., and J. Beck (2001), *Attention Economy*, Harvard Business School Press, Cambridge, Mass.

Liebowitz, J. (2006), *Strategic Intelligence: Business Intelligence, Competitive Intelligence, and Knowledge Management*, Auerbach Publishers/Taylor & Francis, New York.

Spira, J., and J. Feintuch (2005), "The Cost of Not Paying Attention: How Interruptions Impact Knowledge Worker Productivity," *KMWorld Magazine*, www.kmworld.com, Information Today Publishing, Medford, N.J.

Appendix A

Knowledge Access and Sharing Survey

A key part of developing a knowledge management strategy is to find out how people gain access to and share knowledge throughout the organization. This survey seeks to gather fairly detailed information about the ways in which you access, share, and use knowledge resources in your work. In answering the questions below, please keep in mind the following: answer for yourself, not how you think someone else in your job might answer, and answer for how you *actually* work now, not how you wish you worked or think you should work.

We expect that some questions will require you to think carefully about the nature of the tasks you perform and how you interact with people both inside and outside the organization on a day-to-day basis. Carefully completing this survey will probably take about 20 minutes. *We appreciate your effort in helping us meet a strategic goal designed to make the organization more effective and to make it easier for all of us to do our jobs on a daily basis.*

Please forward your completed survey to _____ via e-mail _____ by ____ 2006. Thank you!

PLEASE PROVIDE THE FOLLOWING INFORMATION:

Name:

Which division are you a part of?

How long have you been a full-time employee in the organization?

- Less than 6 months
- 6 months to less than 1 year

- 1 year to less than 3 years
- 3 years to less than 5 years
- More than 5 years

1. In the course of doing your job, which resource do you most often turn to *first* when looking for information? (Please check only one.)
   - E-mail or talk to a colleague in the organization
   - E-mail or talk to a colleague who works outside the organization
   - Do a global web search (for example, Google or Yahoo)
   - Go to a known website
   - Search online organization resources (for example on the intranet)
   - Search through documents/publications in your office
   - Post a message on a Listserv/online community to which you belong
   - Ask your manager for guidance based on his/her experience
   - Other (please specify)
2. What would be your second course of action from the above list?
3. Think about the times when you've been really frustrated by not having a crucial piece of knowledge or information you needed to get something done at the organization. Give an example, including the nature of the challenge and how the need eventually was met.

KNOWLEDGE RESOURCES

4. How often **on average** do you use each of the following to do your job (daily, weekly, monthly, quarterly, or never)?
   - Organization-wide database
   - Organization-operated website (e.g., an intranet)
   - Department- or division-operated database (e.g., shared calendar)
   - My own database or contact list file
   - Organization policy/procedures manual or guidelines
   - Department- or division-specific procedures manual or guidelines
   - Vendor-provided procedures manual or guidelines
   - My own notes or procedures
5. List up to five resources (hard copy or web based) that you use to perform your job and indicate how often you use them. These resources can be journals, magazines, newsletters, books, websites, and so forth. (Specify whether you use each resource daily, weekly, monthly, or quarterly.)
6. How often **on average** do you ask each of the following employees for help with understanding or clarifying how to perform your job, solve a

problem, get an answer to a question from a customer, or learn how to accomplish a new task (daily, weekly, monthly, quarterly, or never)?
- Your immediate supervisor
- Your department head
- Your division head
- Subject matter expert (in an area of policy, practice, or research)
- Technical or functional expert (e.g., accounting, legal, or contracts administration)
  - A peer or colleague in your department or division (informal)
  - A peer or colleague outside your department of division (informal)
7. Name the top three people, in order, to whom you go when you have questions or seek advice in the following areas:
   - General advice
   - Management and leadership knowledge/advice
   - Subject-matter expertise/content knowledge
   - Institutional/historical knowledge
   - Technical/procedural knowledge
8. List up to five experts *outside* the organization you contact to do your job. For each one, please indicate how often **on average** you contact them (daily, weekly, monthly, or quarterly).

KNOWLEDGE USE

9. Which of the following do you *usually* use and/or perform (that is, on a daily or weekly basis) in doing your job? (Check all that apply.)
   - Data or information from a known source (e.g., database or files) you have to retrieve to answer a specific question
   - Data or information you have to gather yourself from multiple sources and analyze and/or synthesize to answer a specific question
   - Step-by-step instructions you provide (that is, not a document) to a customer, vendor, or staff person
   - Direction you provide to a customer, vendor, or staff person (such as advice, counsel, or guidance, not step-by-step instructions)
   - Judgments or recommendations you are asked to make based on data or information that is given to you
   - Judgments or recommendations you are asked to make based on data or information that you must find yourself
   - Routine procedure or process for handling information, paperwork, requests, payments, invoices, and so forth (always done the same way)

- Variable procedure or process for handling information, paperwork, requests, payments, invoices, and so forth (requires some analysis and judgment to select the proper procedure or process to follow)
- Reports, memoranda, letters, or informational materials for customers, vendors, or staff that you must compile and/or write
- Educational or promotional materials that you must compile and/or write
- Proposals you develop to recommend new programs, projects, procedures, or processes

10. After you have received, gathered, or produced information, instructions, documents, proposals, etc., and completed the task, what do you do with them? (Check all that apply.)
    - Save them in an electronic file in my personal directory
    - Save them in an electronic file in a shared directory (e.g., s: drive on an intranet)
    - Save them in a personal paper file
    - Save them in a secure departmental paper file
    - Save them in an open departmental paper file
    - Share them or distribute them to others
    - Delete or toss them
    - Other (please specify)

SHARING

11. When you come across a news item, article, magazine, book, website, announcement for a meeting or course, or some other information that may be useful to other organization staff, what are you *most likely* to do? (Check only one.)
    - Tell them about it or distribute a copy to them personally
    - Post an announcement on the intranet
    - Send a broadcast e-mail
    - Send a memo or a copy through the interoffice mail
    - Intend to share it but usually too busy to follow through
    - Include it in the weekly update
    - Ignore it
    - Other (please specify)

12. What are the constraints you face in being able to access or share knowledge?

13. What crucial knowledge is at risk of being lost in your department or division because of turnover and lack of back-up expertise?

TRAINING/TOOLS

14. When you want to learn or improve a skill or task, what do you prefer to do? (Check all that apply.)
    * Get formal face-to-face training or coursework outside the workplace
    * Get formal self-directed training (e.g., workbook, CD-ROM, or online course)
    * Have a specialist train me onsite
    * Train myself (informally, using a manual or tutorial program)
    * Have my supervisor show me how to do it
    * Have a friend or colleague show me how to do it
    * Other (please specify)

15. What kind of tools or resources do you prefer to help you do your job? (Check all that apply.)
    * Person I can talk to in real time
    * Help line or help desk via phone, fax, or e-mail
    * Advice via online communities of practice (on the intranet, Listservs, or other sources)
    * Printed documents (for example, resource books, manuals)
    * Electronic documents
    * Audiovisual/multimedia material
    * Special software
    * Web-based utility, directory, or service
    * Other (please specify)

KNOWLEDGE NEEDS

16. What information or knowledge that *you* don't currently have would you like to have to do your job better? Consider all aspects of your job, including administrative tasks, policies and procedures, and interpersonal relationships.

17. What information or knowledge that *the organization* currently does not have do you think it should or will need to have to execute its mission, improve organizational effectiveness, and serve its customers with excellence? (You may answer for specific departments as well as for the organization as a whole.)

18. To what extent do you agree with the following statements (strongly disagree, disagree, no opinion, agree, or strongly agree)?
    * I would benefit from having access to documents that contain introductory knowledge that I currently have to acquire from experts directly.

- I would benefit from templates to help me more easily capture knowledge (e.g., standard format for documenting what I learned at a conference or meeting).
- I would benefit from processes to help me contribute knowledge that I don't currently document or share.
- I would benefit from support to determine the most relevant knowledge to share for various audiences and how best to share it.
- I have knowledge in areas that I know the organization could benefit from but no way to make it available.

KNOWLEDGE FLOW

19. Imagine that you've just won your organization's first Knowledge Sharing Award. This award is given to a person who shares his or her mission- or operation-critical knowledge so that the organization can be more effective. List the top five categories of knowledge that earned you this award and the category of staff with whom you shared it.
20. How can the knowledge flow in your area of responsibility be improved?

ADDITIONAL COMMENTS

Thank you for taking the time to complete this survey.

Appendix B

GAO Report on Human Capital

Report to Congressional Requesters, September 2003
Human Capital: Insights for U.S. Agencies from Other Countries' Succession
   Planning and Management Initiatives
GAO-03-914 9 (available in PDF format at http://www.gao.gov/ as GAO-03-
   914)
Highlights of GAO-03-914, a Report to Congressional Requesters

WHY GAO DID THIS STUDY

Leading public organizations here and abroad recognize that a more strategic approach to human capital management is essential for change initiatives that are intended to transform their cultures. To that end, organizations are looking for ways to identify and develop the leaders, managers, and workforce necessary to face the array of challenges that will confront government in the 21st century. GAO conducted this study to identify how agencies in four countries—Australia, Canada, New Zealand, and the United Kingdom—are adopting a more strategic approach to managing the succession of senior executives and other public sector employees with critical skills. These agencies' experiences may provide insights to executive branch agencies as they undertake their own succession planning and management initiatives.

   GAO identified the examples described in this report through discussions with officials from central human capital agencies, national audit offices, and agencies in Australia, Canada, New Zealand, and the United Kingdom, and a screening survey sent to senior human capital officials at selected agencies.

WHAT GAO FOUND

Leading organizations engage in broad, integrated succession planning and management efforts that focus on strengthening both current and future organizational capacity. As part of this approach, these organizations identify, develop, and select their human capital to ensure that successors are the right people, with the right skills, at the right time for leadership and other key positions. To this end, agencies in Australia, Canada, New Zealand, and the United Kingdom are implementing succession planning and management initiatives that are designed to protect and enhance organizational capacity. Collectively, these agencies' initiatives demonstrated the practices shown below.

SELECTED PRACTICES USED BY AGENCIES IN OTHER COUNTRIES TO MANAGE SUCCESSION

- Receive active support of top leadership. Top leadership actively participates in, regularly uses, and ensures the needed financial and staff resources for key succession planning and management initiatives. For example, New Zealand's State Services Commissioner developed, with the assistance of a group of six agency chief executives who met regularly over a period of 2 years, a new governmentwide senior leadership and management development strategy.
- Link to strategic planning. To focus on both current and future needs and to provide leaders with a broader perspective, the Royal Canadian Mounted Police's succession planning and management initiative figures prominently in the agency's multiyear human capital plan and provides top leaders with an agencywide perspective when making decisions.
- Identify talent from multiple organizational levels, early in careers, or with critical skills. For example, the United Kingdom's Fast Stream program specifically targets high-potential individuals early in their civil service careers as well as those recently graduated from college with the aim of providing them with experiences and training linked to strengthening specific competencies required for admission to the Senior Civil Service.
- Emphasize developmental assignments in addition to formal training. Initiatives emphasize developmental assignments in addition to formal training to strengthen high-potential employees' skills and broaden their experience. For example, Canada's Accelerated Executive Development Program temporarily assigns executives to work in unfamiliar roles or subject areas, and in different agencies.

- Address specific human capital challenges, such as diversity, leadership capacity, and retention. For example, the United Kingdom created a centralized program that targets minorities with the potential to join the Senior Civil Service. To help retain high-potential employees, Canada's Office of the Auditor General provides comprehensive developmental opportunities.
- Facilitate broader transformation efforts. To find individuals to champion recent changes in how it delivers services and interacts with stakeholders, the Family Court of Australia identifies and prepares future leaders who will have the skills and experiences to help the organization successfully adapt to agency transformation.

(www.gao.gov/cgi-bin/getrpt?GAO-03-914)
To view the full product, including the scope and methodology, click on the link above. For more information, contact J. Christopher Mihm at (202) 512-6806 or mihmj@gao.gov. A letter dated September 15, 2003:

The Honorable Jo Ann Davis
Chairwoman, Subcommittee on Civil Service and Agency Organization
Committee on Government Reform
House of Representatives

The Honorable George V. Voinovich
Chairman, Subcommittee on Oversight of Government Management, the Federal Workforce, and the District of Columbia
Committee on Governmental Affairs
United States Senate

Leading public organizations here and abroad recognize that a more strategic approach to managing human capital should be the centerpiece of any serious change management initiative to transform the cultures of government agencies. Such organizations recognize that they need both senior leaders who are drivers of continuous improvement and who stimulate and support efforts to integrate human capital approaches with organizational goals, as well as a dynamic, results-oriented workforce with the requisite talents, knowledge, and skills to ensure that they are equipped to achieve organizational missions.[1] Leading organizations are looking for ways to identify and develop the leaders, managers, and workforce necessary to face the array of challenges that will confront government in the 21st century.

We are seeing increased attention to strategic human capital management and a real and growing momentum for change. The Congress required agencies in the federal government to establish a chief human capital officer in legislation creating the Department of Homeland Security enacted in November 2002.[2] One of the officer's functions is to align the agency's human capital policies and programs with organizational mission, strategic goals, and performance outcomes. We have reported that some U.S. agencies have begun to take steps to more closely integrate their human capital and strategic planning processes and hold both human capital professionals and operational managers accountable for accomplishing organizational missions and program goals.[3] More recently, the Office of Management and Budget revised Circular A-11 to require that federal agencies' fiscal year 2005 budget submissions as well as their annual performance plans prepared under the Government Performance and Results Act identify specific activities such as training, development, and staffing that agencies plan to take to ensure leadership continuity. In addition, as part of the Administration's efforts to implement the President's Management Agenda, the Office of Personnel Management (OPM) set the goal that continuity of leadership and knowledge is assured through succession planning and professional development programs in 25 percent of all federal agencies by July 2004. OPM also identified the need for agencies to reduce any current or future skill gaps in mission critical occupations and leadership positions.

We previously reported that other countries have faced challenges in managing their human capital and, in particular, managing individual performance.[4] In addition, other countries face a variety of succession-related challenges. For example, Canada faces a public service workforce with about 80 percent of both its executives and executive feeder groups eligible to retire by the end of the decade. The United Kingdom faces the challenge of increasing the representation of ethnic minorities among its senior executives and has established a goal of doubling the percentage of minority representation from 1.6 percent in 1998 to 3.2 percent by 2005. New Zealand found that past arrangements for the governmentwide development of its senior leaders have not worked, resulting in a shortage of fully prepared candidates for public service leadership positions. To address this shortage, the government has recently launched a new strategic senior leadership and management development initiative. Finally, Australia's central federal human capital agency recently reported on the changing career expectations among employees and the possible attrition of experienced high-potential employees as two succession-related challenges to government performance in the future.

At your request, this report identifies how agencies in four countries— Australia, Canada, New Zealand, and the United Kingdom—and the Canadian Province of Ontario are adopting a more strategic approach to managing the succession of senior executives and other public sector employees with critical skills. To identify these practices, we reviewed the literature associated with succession planning and management; found examples illustrating these practices through the results of a screening survey; analyzed written documentation; and interviewed cognizant officials about the identified examples. See appendix I for additional information on our objective, scope, and methodology.

RESULTS IN BRIEF

Leading organizations engage in broad, integrated succession planning and management efforts that focus on strengthening both current and future organizational capacity. As part of this approach, these organizations identify, develop, and select their human capital to ensure an ongoing supply of successors who are the right people, with the right skills, at the right time for leadership and other key positions. Agencies in Australia, Canada, New Zealand, and the United Kingdom are implementing succession planning and management initiatives that reflect this broader focus on building organizational capacity.

While each initiative reflects its specific organizational structure, culture, and priorities, collectively we found that agencies in these countries use the succession planning and management practices to protect and enhance the organization's capacity. Their experiences may provide insights to U.S. executive branch agencies as they undertake their own initiatives in this area.

SUCCESSION PLANNING AND MANAGEMENT INITIATIVES

- receive active support of top leadership
- link to strategic planning
- identify talent from multiple organizational levels, early in careers, or with critical skills
- emphasize developmental assignments in addition to formal training
- address specific human capital challenges, such as diversity, leadership capacity, and retention
- facilitate broader transformation efforts

First, to show their support for succession planning and management, agencies' top leadership actively participate in, regularly use, and ensure the needed financial and staff resources for these initiatives. For example, New Zealand's State Services Commissioner developed, with the assistance of a group of six agency chief executives who met regularly over a period of 2 years, a new governmentwide senior leadership and management development strategy. In the Ontario Public Service, the government's top civil servant and the heads of every ministry meet for an annual 2-day retreat to discuss anticipated leadership needs across the government as well as the high-potential executives who may be able to meet those needs over the next year or two.

Second, agencies link succession planning and management with their strategic plans to focus on both current and future needs and provide leaders with a broader perspective. For the Royal Canadian Mounted Police, succession planning and management not only figures prominently in the agency's multiyear human capital plan, but it also provides top agency leaders with an agencywide perspective when making decisions. To this end, the agency uses a specially designated "succession room" to provide a visual representation of the agency's diverse and widely dispersed operational functions, which assists top leadership in placing and tracking executives and managers across organizational structures.

Third, agencies use their succession planning and management initiatives to identify talent at multiple organizational levels, early in their careers, or with critical skills. For example, the Royal Canadian Mounted Police has three separate programs to identify and develop high-potential employees at several organizational levels reaching as far down as the front-line constable. The United Kingdom's Fast Stream program targets high-potential individuals early in their careers. Other agencies use their succession management initiatives to identify and develop successors for employees with critical knowledge and skills. Transport Canada anticipated that the retirements of key regulatory inspectors would severely affect the agency's ability to carry out its mandate. The agency encouraged the use of human capital flexibilities, such as preretirement transitional leave, to help ensure a smooth transition of knowledge from incumbents to successors.

Fourth, agencies' succession planning and management initiatives emphasize developmental assignments in addition to formal training to strengthen high-potential employees' skills and broaden their experience. For example, Canada's Accelerated Executive Development Program temporarily assigns executives who have the potential to become assistant deputy ministers to work in unfamiliar roles or subject areas and in different agencies. One challenge sometimes encountered with developmental assignments in general is that agencies resist letting their high-potential staff leave their current positions to move to another organization. The Accelerated Executive Development Program has addressed this challenge by having a central government agency pay participants' salaries, which makes executives more willing to allow talented staff to leave for developmental assignments. New Zealand has responded to this challenge by appropriating funds to help defray the costs to backfill positions for individuals on developmental assignments.

Fifth, agencies use their succession planning and management initiatives to address specific human capital challenges such as achieving a more diverse workforce, maintaining leadership capacity, and increasing the retention of high-potential employees. For example, the United Kingdom created and has actively marketed a centralized program that targets minorities with the potential to join the Senior Civil Service. To help maintain leadership capacity despite the fact that three quarters of Canada's assistant deputy ministers will be retirement eligible by 2008, the Canadian government uses the Accelerated Executive Development Program to identify and develop executives with the potential to effectively fill these positions in the future. To better retain talented employees with the potential to become future leaders, Canada's Office of the Auditor General provides comprehensive developmental opportunities as part of its succession planning and management initiative.

Finally, agencies use succession planning and management to facilitate broader transformation efforts by selecting and developing leaders and managers who support and champion change. For example, the Family Court of Australia is using its succession planning and management initiative to identify and prepare future leaders who will be able to help the organization successfully adapt to recent changes in how it delivers its services, and then champion those changes throughout the Court. In the United Kingdom, an official told us that the National Health Service uses its succession planning and management initiative to select and place executives who will champion broader organizational reform efforts.

We provided drafts of the relevant sections of this report to officials from the central agencies responsible for human capital issues, the individual agencies, and the national audit offices for each of the countries we reviewed, as well as subject matter experts in the United States. They generally agreed with the contents of this report. We made technical clarifications where appropriate. We also provided a draft of this report to the Director of OPM for her information.

BACKGROUND

Many federal agencies have yet to adopt succession planning and management initiatives. In 1997, the National Academy of Public Administration reported that of the 27 agencies responding to its survey, 2 agencies had a succession planning program or process in place; 2 agencies were planning to have one in the coming year; and 4 agencies were planning one in the next 2 years.[5] In 1999, a joint OPM and Senior Executive Association survey reported that more than 50 percent of all career members of the Senior Executive Service (SES) said that their agencies did not have a formal succession planning program for the SES, and almost 75 percent said that their agencies did not have such a program for managers.[6] Of those who reported that their agencies did have succession planning programs for either executives or managers, 54 percent of the career senior executives said that they had not participated in the executive-level programs and 65 percent said they had not participated at the manager level. On the basis of this survey and anecdotal evidence, OPM officials told us in 2000 that they found that most agencies would not likely have a formal, comprehensive succession plan.[7]

Further, we have reported that a lack of succession planning has contributed to two specific human capital challenges currently facing the federal government. The first challenge is the large percentage of career senior executives who will reach regular retirement eligibility over the next several years. In 2000, we reported that 71 percent of the SES members employed as of October 1998 would reach regular retirement eligibility by the end of fiscal year 2005.[8] More recently, we estimated that more than half of the SES members in federal service as of October 2000 will have left the government by October 2007.[9] We concluded that without careful planning, these separations pose the threat of an eventual loss in institutional knowledge, expertise, and leadership continuity.

The second challenge facing federal agencies impacted by a lack of succession planning is the amount of diversity in their executive and managerial ranks. As the demographics of the public served by the federal government change, a diverse executive corps can provide agencies with an increasingly important organizational advantage that can help them to achieve results. We have reported that, as of 2000, minority men and women made up about 14 percent of the career SES. If current promotion and hiring trends continue, the proportions of minority men and women among senior executives will likely remain virtually unchanged over the next 4 years.[10]

The literature shows that public and private sector organizations use a range of approaches when planning for, and managing, succession-related challenges. These approaches span a continuum from the "replacement" approach, which focuses on identifying particular individuals as possible successors for specific top ranking positions, to the "integrated" succession planning and management approach. Under the integrated approach, succession planning and management is a strategic, systematic effort that works to ensure a suitable supply of potential successors for a variety of leadership and other key positions. These two approaches essentially reflect a shift in emphasis of succession planning from a risk management tool, focused on the near-term, operational need to ensure backup people are identified in case a top position becomes vacant, to a strategic planning tool, which identifies and develops high-potential individuals with the aim of filling leadership and other key roles in the future.

GAO, similar to other federal agencies, faces an array of succession planning challenges. The succession planning and management approach we are using to respond to our internal challenges is consistent with the practices we identified in other countries.

OTHER COUNTRIES' SELECTED PRACTICES TO MANAGE SUCCESSION

To manage the succession of their executives and other key employees, agencies in Australia, Canada, New Zealand, and the United Kingdom are implementing succession planning and management practices that work to protect and enhance organizational capacity. Collectively, these agencies' succession planning and management initiatives

- Receive active support of top leadership
- Link to strategic planning
- Identify talent from multiple organizational levels, early in careers, or with critical skills
- Emphasize developmental assignments in addition to formal training
- Address specific human capital challenges, such as diversity, leadership capacity, and retention
- Facilitate broader transformation efforts

RECEIVE ACTIVE SUPPORT OF TOP LEADERSHIP

Effective succession planning and management programs have the support and commitment of their organizations' top leadership. Our past work has shown that the demonstrated commitment of top leaders is perhaps the single most important element of successful management.[11] In other governments and agencies, to demonstrate its support of succession planning and management, top leadership (1) actively participates in the initiatives, (2) regularly uses these programs to develop, place, and promote individuals, and (3) ensures that these programs receive sufficient financial and staff resources, and are maintained over time.

For example, each year, the Secretary of the Cabinet, Ontario Public Service's (OPS) top civil servant, convenes and actively participates in an annual 2-day succession planning and management retreat with the heads of every government ministry. At this retreat, they discuss the anticipated leadership needs across the government as well as the individual status of about 200 high-potential executives who may be able to meet those needs over the next year or two. Similarly, in New Zealand, the State Services Commissioner—an official whose wide-ranging human capital responsibilities include the appointment and review of public service chief executives—developed, with the assistance of a group of six agency chief executives who met regularly over a period of 2 years, a new governmentwide senior leadership and management development initiative. This effort culminated in the July 2003 roll out of the Executive Leadership Programme and the creation of a new central Leadership Development Centre.

The Royal Canadian Mounted Police's (RCMP) senior executive committee regularly uses the agency's succession planning and management programs when making decisions to develop, place, and promote its top 500–600 employees, both officers and civilians. RCMP's executive committee, consisting of the agency's chief executive, the chief human capital officer, and six other top officials, meets quarterly to discuss the organization's succession needs and to make the specific decisions concerning individual staff necessary to address those needs. In 2001–2002, this process resulted in 72 promotions and 220 lateral transfers.

Top leaders also demonstrate support by ensuring that their agency's or government's succession planning and management initiatives receive sufficient funding and staff resources necessary to operate effectively and are maintained over time. Such commitment is critical since these initiatives can be expensive because of the emphasis they place on participant development. For example, a senior human capital manager told us that the Chief Executive of the Family Court of Australia (FCA) pledged to earmark funds when he established a multiyear succession planning and management program in 2002 despite predictions of possible budget cuts facing FCA. Although human capital training and development programs are sometimes among the first programs to be cut back during periods of retrenchment, FCA's Chief Executive has repeatedly stated to both internal and external stakeholders that this will not happen.

Similarly, at Statistics Canada—the Canadian federal government's central statistics agency—the Chief Statistician of Canada has set aside a percentage, in this case over 3 percent, of the total agency budget to training and development, thus making resources available for the operation of the agency's four leadership and management development programs. According to a human capital official, this strong support has enabled the level of funding to remain fairly consistent over the past 10 years. Finally, the government of New Zealand has committed NZ$19.6 million (about US$11.2 million in July 2003) over four years, representing both central government and agency contributions, for the implementation of its new governmentwide senior leadership and management development strategy.

LINK TO STRATEGIC PLANNING

Leading organizations use succession planning and management as a strategic planning tool that focuses on current and future needs and develops pools of high-potential staff in order to meet the organization's mission over the long term. That is, succession planning and management is used to help the organization become what it needs to be, rather than simply to recreate the existing organization. We have previously reported on the importance of linking succession planning and management with the forward-looking process of strategic and program planning.[12] In Canada, succession planning and management initiatives focus on long-term goals, are closely integrated with their strategic plans, and provide a broader perspective.

For example, at Statistics Canada, committees composed of line and senior managers and human capital specialists consider the human capital required to achieve its strategic goals and objectives. During the 2001 strategic planning process, the agency's planning committees received projections showing that a majority of the senior executives then in place would retire by 2010, and the number of qualified assistant directors in the executive development pool was insufficient to replace them. In response, the agency increased the size of the pool and introduced a development program of training, rotation, and mentoring to expedite the development of those already in the pool. According to a Statistics Canada human capital official, these actions, linked with the agency's strategic planning process, have helped to ensure that an adequate number of assistant directors will be sufficiently prepared to succeed departing senior executives.

In Ontario, succession planning and management has been a required component of the government's human capital planning framework since 1997. OPS requires that the head of each ministry develop a succession plan that (1) anticipates the ministry's needs over the next couple of years, (2) establishes a process to identify a pool of high-potential senior managers, and (3) links the selection of possible successors to both ministry and governmentwide opportunities and business plans. These plans, which are updated annually at the deputy ministers retreat, form the basis for Ontario's governmentwide succession planning and management process. While OPS has not conducted a formal evaluation of the impact of this process, a senior human capital official told us that succession planning and management has received a much greater level of attention from top leadership and now plays a critical role in OPS' broader planning and staffing efforts.

For RCMP, succession planning and management is an integral part of the agency's multiyear human capital plan and directly supports its strategic needs, and it also uses this process to provide top leadership with an agency-wide perspective. RCMP is responsible for a wide range of police functions on the federal, provincial, and local levels, such as illegal drug and border enforcement, international peacekeeping services, and road and highway safety. In addition, RCMP provides services in 10 provinces and three territories covering an area larger than the United States. Its succession planning and management system provides the RCMP Commissioner and his executive committee with an organizationwide picture of current and developing leadership capacity across the organization's many functional and geographic lines.

To achieve this, RCMP constructed a "succession room"—a dedicated room with a graphic representation of current and potential job positions for the organization's top 500–600 employees covering its walls—where the Commissioner and his top executives meet at least four times a year to discuss succession planning and management for the entire organization. For each of RCMP's executive and senior manager–level positions in headquarters and the regions, the incumbent and one or more potential successors are depicted on individual movable cards that display relevant background information. . . . An electronic database provides access to more detailed information for each incumbent and potential successors, including skills, training, and past job experience that the executive committee considers when deciding on assignments and transfers. In addition, high-potential individuals as well as employees currently on developmental assignments outside RCMP are displayed. According to a senior human capital official, because the succession room actually surrounds the RCMP's top leadership with an accessible depiction of their complex and wide-ranging organization, it provides a powerful tool to help them take a broader, organizationwide approach to staffing and management decisions.

IDENTIFY TALENT FROM MULTIPLE ORGANIZATIONAL LEVELS, EARLY IN CAREERS, OR WITH CRITICAL SKILLS

Effective succession planning and management initiatives identify high-performing employees from multiple levels in the organization and still early in their careers. In addition, leading organizations use succession planning and management to identify and develop knowledge and skills that are critical in the workplace.

RCMP has three separate development programs that identify and develop high-potential employees at several organizational levels. For example, beginning at entry level, the Full Potential Program reaches as far down as the front-line constable and identifies and develops individuals, both civilians and officers, who demonstrate the potential to take on a future management role. For more experienced staff, RCMP's Officer Candidate Development Program identifies and prepares individuals for increased leadership and managerial responsibilities and to successfully compete for admission to the officer candidate pool. Finally, RCMP's Senior Executive Development Process helps to identify successors for the organization's senior executive corps by selecting and developing promising officers for potential promotion to the senior executive levels.

The United Kingdom's Fast Stream program targets high-potential individuals early in their civil service careers as well as recent college graduates. The program places participants in a series of jobs designed to provide experiences such as developing policy, supporting ministers, and managing people and projects—each of which is linked to strengthening specific competencies required for admission to the Senior Civil Service. According to a senior program official, program participants are typically promoted quickly, attaining mid-level management in an average of 3.5 years, and the Senior Civil Service in about 7 years after that.

Other agencies use their succession planning and management initiatives to identify and develop successors for employees with critical knowledge and skills. For example, Transport Canada estimated that 69 percent of its safety and security regulatory employees, including inspectors, are eligible for retirement by 2008. Faced with the urgent need to capture and pass on the inspectors' expertise, judgment, and insights before they retire, the agency embarked on a major knowledge management initiative in 1999 as part of its succession planning and management activities. To identify the inspectors whose leaving would most severely affect the agency's ability to carry out its mandate, Transport Canada used criteria that assessed whether the inspectors (1) possessed highly specialized knowledge, skills, or expertise, (2) held one-of-a-kind positions, (3) were regarded as the "go-to" people in critical situations, and/or (4) held vital corporate memory. Next, inspectors were asked to pass on their knowledge through mentoring, coaching, and on-the-job training. To assist this knowledge transfer effort, Transport Canada encouraged these inspectors to use human capital flexibilities including preretirement transitional leave, which allows employees to substantially reduce their workweek without reducing pension and benefits payments. The Treasury Board of Canada Secretariat, a federal central management agency, found that besides providing easy access to highly specialized knowledge, this initiative ensures a smooth transition of knowledge from incumbents to successors.

EMPHASIZE DEVELOPMENTAL ASSIGNMENTS
IN ADDITION TO FORMAL TRAINING

Leading succession planning and management initiatives emphasize developmental or "stretch" assignments for high-potential employees in addition to formal training. These developmental assignments place staff in new roles or unfamiliar job environments in order to strengthen skills and competencies and broaden their experience. In the United States, training and development opportunities—including developmental assignments—must be offered fairly, consistent with merit system principles. However, according to a 1999 survey of career SES in the United States, 67 percent reported that they had never changed jobs by going to a different component within their agency or department. Moreover, 91 percent said that they never served in more than one department or agency during their entire executive careers.[13] Agencies in other countries use developmental assignments, accompanied by more formal training components and other support mechanisms, to help ensure that individuals are capable of performing when promoted.

Participants in RCMP's Full Potential Program must complete at least two 6- to 12-month developmental assignments intended to enhance specific competencies identified in their personalized development plans. These assignments provide participants with the opportunity to learn new skills and apply existing skills in different situations and experience an increased level of authority, responsibility, and accountability. For example, a civilian from technical operations and a police officer were given a 1-year assignment to create balanced scorecards that are linked to RCMP's goals. Another program assignment involved placing a line officer, previously in charge of a single RCMP unit, in the position of acting district commander responsible for the command of multiple units during a period of resource and financial constraint. To reinforce the learning that comes from the developmental assignments, participants attend a 6-week educational program provided by Canada's Centre for Management and Development that covers the personal, interpersonal, managerial, and organizational dimensions of leadership. Each participant also benefits from the support and professional expertise of a senior-level mentor. Staff who complete this program will be required to continue their formal development as RCMP officer candidates.

In Canada's Accelerated Executive Development Program (AEXDP), developmental assignments form the cornerstone of efforts to prepare senior executives for top leadership roles in the public service. Canada created AEXDP in 1997 to strategically manage the development of senior executives who have the potential to become assistant deputy ministers within 2 to 6 years. AEXDP prepares individuals for these senior leadership positions through the support of coaches and mentors, formal learning events, and placements in a series of challenging developmental assignments. These stretch assignments help enhance executive competencies by having participants perform work in areas that are unfamiliar or challenging to them in any of a large number of agencies throughout the Canadian Public Service. For example, a participant with a background in policy could develop his or her managerial competencies through an assignment to manage a direct service delivery program in a different agency. Central to the benefit of such assignments is that they provide staff with the opportunity to practice new skills in a real-time setting. Further, each assignment lasts approximately 2 years, which allows time for participants to maximize their learning experience while providing agencies with sufficient opportunity to gain a real benefit from the participants' contributions.

AEXDP reinforces the learning provided by the developmental assignments with activities such as "action learning groups" where small groups of five or six program participants meet periodically to collectively reflect on and address actual work situations or challenges facing individual participants. A senior official involved in the program told us that the developmental placements help participants obtain in-depth experience in how other organizations make decisions and solve problems, while simultaneously developing a governmentwide network of contacts that they can call on for expertise and advice in the future.

One challenge sometimes encountered with developmental assignments in general is that executives and managers resist letting their high-potential staff leave their current positions to move to another organization. Agencies in other countries have developed several approaches to respond to this challenge. For example, once individuals are accepted into Canada's AEXDP, they are employees of, and paid by, the Public Service Commission, a central agency. Officials affiliated with AEXDP told us that not having to pay participants' salaries makes executives more willing to allow talented staff to leave for developmental assignments and it fosters a governmentwide, rather than an agency-specific, culture among the AEXDP participants.

In New Zealand, a senior official at the State Services Commission, the central agency responsible for ensuring that agencies develop public service leadership capability, told us that the Commission has recommended legislation that would require that agency chief executives work in partnership with the State Services Commissioner to find ways to release talented people for external developmental assignments. In addition, the government has appropriated NZ$600,000 (about US$344,000 in July 2003) over the next 4 years to help the Commissioner assist agency chief executives who might like to release an individual for a developmental assignment but are inhibited from doing so because of financial constraints, including those associated with finding a replacement.

ADDRESS SPECIFIC HUMAN CAPITAL CHALLENGES

Leading organizations stay alert to human capital challenges and respond accordingly. Government agencies around the world, including in the United States, are facing challenges in the demographic makeup and diversity of their senior executives. Agencies in other countries use succession planning and management to achieve a more diverse workforce, maintain their leadership capacity as their senior executives retire, and increase the retention of high-potential staff.

Achieve a More Diverse Workforce. Leading organizations recognize that diversity can be an organizational strength that contributes to achieving results. Our work has shown that U.S. federal agencies will need to enhance their efforts to improve diversity as the SES turns over.[14] In addition, OPM has identified an increase in workforce diversity, including in mission critical occupations and leadership roles, as one of its human capital management goals for implementing the President's Management Agenda. Both the United Kingdom and Canada use succession planning and management systems to address the challenge of increasing the diversity of their senior executive corps.

For example, the United Kingdom's Cabinet Office created Pathways, a 2-year program that identifies and develops senior managers from ethnic minorities who have the potential to reach the Senior Civil Service within 3 to 5 years. This program is intended to achieve a governmentwide goal to double the representation of ethnic minorities in the Senior Civil Service from 1.6 percent in 1998 to 3.2 percent by 2005. Pathways provides executive coaching, skills training, and the chance for participants to demonstrate their potential and talent through a variety of developmental activities such as projects and short-term work placements. A Cabinet Office official told us that the program is actively marketed through a series of nationwide informational meetings held in locations with large ethnic minority populations. In addition, program information is sent to government agency chief executives and human capital directors, and the top 600 senior executives across the civil service, and executives are encouraged to supplement the self-nominating process by nominating potential candidates. This official noted that although the first Pathways class will not graduate until November 2003, 2 out of the 20 participants have already been promoted to the Senior Civil Service.

Rather than a specific program, Canada uses AEXDP, an essential component of their succession planning and management process for senior executives, as a tool to help achieve a governmentwide diversity target. For example, the government has set a goal that by 2003, certain minorities will represent 20 percent of participants in all management development programs. After conducting a survey of minorities, who showed a considerable level of interest in the program, officials from AEXDP devoted 1 year's recruitment efforts to identify and select qualified minorities. The program reported that, in the three prior AEXDP classes, such minorities represented 4.5 percent of the total number of participants; however, by March 2002, AEXDP achieved the goal of 20 percent minority participation. In addition, an independent evaluation by an outside consulting firm found that the percentage of these minorities participating in AEXDP is more than three times the percentage in the general senior executive population.

Maintain Leadership Capacity. Both at home and abroad, a large percentage of senior executives will be eligible to retire over the next several years. In the United States, for example, the federal government faces an estimated loss of more than half of the career SES by October 2007.[15] Other countries that face the same demographic trend use succession planning and management to maintain leadership capacity in anticipation of the turnover of their senior executive corps due to expected retirements. Canada is using AEXDP to address impending retirements of assistant deputy ministers—one of the most senior executive-level positions in its civil service. As of February 2003, for example, 76 percent of this group are over 50, and approximately 75 percent are eligible to retire between now and 2008. A recent independent evaluation of AEXDP by an outside consulting firm found the program to be successful and concluded that AEXDP participants are promoted in greater numbers than, and at a significantly accelerated rate over, their nonprogram counterparts. Specifically, of the participants who joined the program at the entry level, 39 percent had been promoted one level and another 7 percent had been promoted two levels within 1 year compared to only 9 percent and 1 percent for nonparticipants during the same period. This evaluation further concluded that AEXDP is a "valuable source" of available senior executives and a "very important source of well-trained, future assistant deputy ministers."

Increase Retention of High-Potential Staff. Canada's Office of the Auditor General (OAG) uses succession planning and management to provide an incentive for high-potential employees to stay with the organization and thus preserve future leadership capacity. Specifically, OAG identified increased retention rates of talented employees as one of the goals of the succession planning and management program it established in 2000. According to a senior human capital official, OAG provided high-potential employees with comprehensive developmental opportunities in order to raise the "exit price" that a competing employer would need to offer to lure a high-potential employee away. The official told us that an individual, who might otherwise have been willing to leave OAG for a salary increase of CN$5,000, might now require CN$10,000 or more, in consideration of the developmental opportunities offered by the agency. Over the program's first 18 months, annualized turnover in OAG's high-potential pool was 6.3 percent compared to 10.5 percent officewide. This official told us that the retention of members of this high-potential pool was key to OAG's efforts to develop future leaders.

FACILITATE BROADER TRANSFORMATION EFFORTS

Effective succession planning and management initiatives provide a potentially powerful tool for fostering broader governmentwide or agencywide transformation by selecting and developing leaders and managers who support and champion change. Our work has shown the critical importance of having top leaders and managers committed to, and personally involved in, implementing management reforms if those reforms are to succeed.[16] Agencies in the United Kingdom and Australia promoted the implementation of broader transformation efforts by using their succession planning and management systems to support new ways of doing business.

In 1999, the United Kingdom launched a wide-ranging reform program known as Modernising Government, which focused on improving the quality, coordination, and accessibility of the services government offered to its citizens. Beginning in 2000, the United Kingdom's Cabinet Office started on a process that continues today of restructuring the content of its leadership and management development programs to reflect this new emphasis on service delivery. For example, the Top Management Programme supports senior executives in developing behaviors and skills for effective and responsive service delivery, and provides the opportunity to discuss and receive expert guidance in topics, tools, and issues associated with the delivery and reform agenda. These programs typically focus on specific areas that have traditionally not been emphasized for executives such as partnerships with the private sector and risk assessment and management. A senior Cabinet Office official responsible for executive development told us that mastering such skills is key to an executive's ability to deliver the results intended in the government's agenda.

The United Kingdom's Department of Health has embarked on a major reform effort involving a 10-year plan to modernize the National Health Service by, among other things, devolving power from the government to the local health services that perform well for their patients, and breaking down occupational boundaries to give staff greater flexibility to provide care. A National Health Service official told us that the service recognizes the key contribution that succession planning and management programs can have and, therefore, selects and places executives who will champion its reform and healthcare service delivery improvement efforts. For example, the Service's National Primary Care Development Team created a leadership development program specifically tailored for clinicians with the expectation that they will, in turn, champion new clinical approaches and help manage the professional and organizational change taking place within the health service.

At the FCA, preparing future leaders who could help the organization successfully adapt to recent changes in how it delivers services is one of the objectives of the agency's Leadership, Excellence, Achievement, Progression program, established in 2002. Specifically, over the last few years FCA has placed an increased emphasis on the needs of external stakeholders. This new emphasis is reflected in the leadership capabilities FCA uses when selecting and developing program participants. For example, one of these capabilities, "nurturing internal and external relationships," emphasizes the importance of taking all stakeholders into account when making decisions, in contrast to the FCA's traditional internally focused culture. In addition, according to a senior human capital manager, individuals selected to participate in the FCA's leadership development program are expected to function as "national drivers of change within the Court." To this end, the program provides participants with a combination of developmental assignments and formal training opportunities that place an emphasis on areas such as project and people management, leadership, and effective change management.

CONCLUDING OBSERVATIONS

As governmental agencies around the world anticipate the need for leaders and other key employees with the necessary competencies to successfully meet the complex challenges of the 21st century, they are choosing succession planning and management initiatives that go beyond simply replacing individuals in order to recreate the existing organization, to initiatives that strategically position the organization for the future. Collectively, the experiences of agencies in Australia, Canada, New Zealand, and the United Kingdom demonstrate how governments are using succession planning and management initiatives that receive the active support of top leadership, link to strategic planning, identify talent throughout the organization, emphasize developmental assignments in addition to formal training, address specific human capital challenges, and facilitate broader transformation efforts. Taken together, these practices give agencies a potentially powerful set of tools with which to strategically manage their most important asset—their human capital.

While there is no one right way for organizations to manage the succession of their leaders and other key employees, the experiences of agencies in these four countries provide insights into how other governments are adopting succession practices that protect and enhance organizational capacity. While governments' and agencies' initiatives reflect their individual organizational structures, cultures, and priorities, these practices can guide executive branch agencies in the United States as they develop their own succession planning and management initiatives in order to ensure that federal agencies have the human capital capacity necessary to achieve their organizational goals and effectively deliver results now and in the future.

AGENCY COMMENTS

We provided drafts of the relevant sections of this report to cognizant officials from the central agency responsible for human capital issues, individual agencies, and the national audit office for each of the countries we reviewed as well as subject matter experts in the United States. They generally agreed with the contents of this report. We made technical clarifications where appropriate. Because we did not evaluate the policies or operations of any U.S. federal agency in this report, we did not seek comments from any U.S. agency. However, because of OPM's role in providing guidance and assistance to federal agencies on succession planning and leadership development, we provided a draft of this report to the Director of OPM for her information.

As agreed with your offices, unless you publicly announce its contents earlier, we plan no further distribution of this report for 30 days from the date of this letter. At that time, we will provide copies of this report to other interested congressional committees, the directors of OPM and the Office of Management and Budget, and the foreign government officials contacted for this report. In addition, we will make copies available to others upon request and the report will be available at no charge on the GAO Web site at [Hyperlink, www.gao.gov] www.gao.gov.

If you have any questions concerning this report, please contact me or Lisa Shames on (202) 512-6806 or at [Hyperlink, mihmj@gao.gov] mihmj@gao.gov and [Hyperlink, shamesl@gao.gov] shamesl@gao.gov. The major contributors to this report were Peter J. Del Toro and Rebecka L. Derr. (J. Christopher Mihm Director, Strategic Issues; signed by J. Christopher Mihm)

APPENDIX I: OBJECTIVE, SCOPE, AND METHODOLOGY

To meet our objective to identify how agencies in other countries are adopting a more strategic approach to managing the succession of senior executives and others with critical skills, we selected Australia, Canada, New Zealand, the United Kingdom, and the Canadian Province of Ontario based on our earlier work where we examined their implementation of results-oriented management and human capital reforms.[17] We reviewed the public management and human capital literature and spoke with subject matter experts to obtain additional context and analysis regarding succession planning and management. A key resource was the National Academy of Public Administration's work on the topic, including their maturity model and subsequent revisions, which describe the major succession planning process elements of initiatives that take a strategic approach to building organizational capacity.[18]

We identified the examples illustrating the practices through the results of over 30 responses to a questionnaire sent to senior human capital officials at selected agencies. We analyzed written documentation including reports, procedures, guidance, and other materials concerning succession planning and management programs for agencies in these countries along with government-sponsored evaluations of these programs when available. We interviewed more than 50 government officials from Australia, Canada, New Zealand, and the United Kingdom by telephone, or in person during a visit to Ottawa, Canada. To obtain a variety of perspectives, we spoke to officials from the countries' national audit offices, central management, and human capital agencies.

The scope of our work did not include independent evaluation or verification of the effectiveness of the succession planning and management initiatives used in the four countries, including any performance results that agencies attributed to specific practices or aspects of their programs. We also did not attempt to assess the prevalence of the practices or challenges we cite either within or across countries. Therefore, countries other than those cited for a particular practice may, or may not, be engaged in the same practice. Because of the multiple jurisdictions covered in this report, we use the term "agency" generically to refer to entities of the central government including departments, ministries, and agencies, except when describing specific examples where we use the term appropriate to that case.

We conducted our work from January through June 2003 in Washington, D.C., and Ottawa, Canada, in accordance with generally accepted government auditing standards. We provided drafts of the relevant sections of this report to officials from the central agencies responsible for human capital issues. individual agencies, and the national audit office for each of the countries we reviewed as well as subject matter experts in the United States. We also provided a draft of this report to the Director of OPM for her information.

NOTES

1. U.S. General Accounting Office, *High-Risk Series: Strategic Human Capital Management*, GAO-03-120 (Washington, D.C.: January 2003).
2. Title XIII of Pub. L. 107-296, Nov. 25, 2002, Chief Human Capital Officers Act of 2002.
3. U.S. General Accounting Office, *Human Capital: Selected Agency Actions to Integrate Human Capital Approaches to Attain Mission Results*, GAO-03-446 (Washington, D.C.: Apr. 11, 2003).
4. U.S. General Accounting Office, *Results-Oriented Cultures: Insights for U.S. Agencies from Other Countries' Performance Management Initiatives*, GAO-02-862 (Washington, D.C.: Aug. 2, 2002).
5. National Academy of Public Administration, *Managing Succession and Developing Leadership: Growing the Next Generation of Public Service Leaders* (Washington, D.C.: August 1997).
6. 1999 OPM/Senior Executive Association Survey of the Senior Executive Service. Complete results of the survey, along with additional background and methodological information, are available on OPM's Web site at www.opm.gov/ses/survey.html.
7. U.S. General Accounting Office, *Senior Executive Service: Retirement Trends Underscore the Importance of Succession Planning*, GAO/GGD-00-113BR (Washington, D.C.: May 12, 2000).
8. GAO/GGD-00-113BR.
9. U.S. General Accounting Office, *Senior Executive Service: Enhanced Agency Efforts Needed to Improve Diversity as the Senior Corps Turns Over*, GAO-03-34 (Washington, D.C.: Jan. 17, 2003).
10. GAO-03-34.
11. U.S. General Accounting Office, *Management Reform: Elements of Successful Improvement Initiatives*, GAO/T-GGD-00-26 (Washington, D.C.: Oct. 15, 1999).
12. U.S. General Accounting Office, *Human Capital: A Self-Assessment Checklist for Agency Leaders*, GAO/OCG-00-14G (Washington, D.C.: September 2000).
13. 1999 OPM/Senior Executive Association Survey of the Senior Executive Service. Complete results on these items as well as other survey questions concerning SES job experience and mobility are available at www.opm.gov/ses/s30.html.
14. GAO-03-34.
15. GAO-03-34.
16. U.S. General Accounting Office, *Results-Oriented Cultures: Using Balanced Expectations to Manage Senior Executive Performance*, GAO-02-966 (Washington,

D.C.: Sept. 27, 2002); *Managing for Results: Using Strategic Human Capital to Drive Transformational Change*, GAO-02-940T (Washington, D.C.: July 15, 2002); and *A Model of Strategic Human Capital Management*, GAO-02-373SP (Washington, D.C.: Mar. 15, 2002).

17. GAO-02-862 and U.S. General Accounting Office, *Managing for Results: Experiences Abroad Suggest Insights for Federal Management Reforms*, GAO/GGD-95-120 (Washington, D.C.: May 2, 1995).

18. See National Academy of Public Administration, *Paths to Leadership: Executive Succession Planning in the Federal Government* (Washington, D.C.: December 1992), *The State of Executive Succession Planning in the Federal Government* (Washington, D.C.: December 1994), and *Managing Succession and Developing Leadership: Growing the Next Generation of Public Service Leaders* (Washington, D.C.: August 1997).

Index

About the Author

Jay Liebowitz is professor of information technology in the Graduate Division of Business and Management at Johns Hopkins University. He is the program director of the Graduate Certificate in Competitive Intelligence at Johns Hopkins University. He is the founder and editor-in-chief of a top-tier refereed journal, *Expert Systems with Applications: An International Journal*, published by Elsevier. Previously, Dr. Liebowitz was the first knowledge management officer at NASA's Goddard Space Flight Center; the Robert W. Deutsch Distinguished Professor of Information Systems at the University of Maryland, Baltimore County; chair of Artificial Intelligence at the U.S. Army War College; and professor of management science at George Washington University. He has published more than thirty books and more than 200 articles dealing with expert/intelligent systems, knowledge management, and information technology management. Dr. Liebowitz edited the first *Knowledge Management Handbook* in 1999. His most recent books are *Addressing the Human Capital Crisis in the Federal Government: A Knowledge Management Perspective* (2004), *Communicating as IT Professionals* (2006), and *Strategic Intelligence: Business Intelligence, Competitive Intelligence, and Knowledge Management* (2006). He is the founder and chair of the World Congress on Expert Systems. Dr. Liebowitz was a Fulbright Scholar, IEEE-USA Federal Communications Commission Executive Fellow, and Computer Educator of the Year (1996). He has consulted and lectured worldwide, and he can be reached at jliebow1@jhu.edu.